The
Practical Tarot
Method

The
Practical Tarot
Method

Learn to Read Tarot Cards Intuitively

LISA KESSLER

BEYOND WORDS
Portland, Oregon

BEYOND WORDS

1750 S.W. Skyline Blvd., Suite 20
Portland, Oregon 97221-2543
503-531-8700 / 503-531-8773 fax
www.beyondword.com

First Beyond Words paperback edition January 2025

BEYOND WORDS PUBLISHING and colophon are registered trademarks of Beyond Words Publishing. Beyond Words is an imprint of Simon & Schuster, LLC.

For more information about special discounts for bulk purchases, please contact Beyond Words Special Sales at 503-531-8700 or specialsales@beyondword.com.

Managing editor: Lindsay Easterbrooks-Brown
Editors: Michele Ashtiani Cohn, Bailey Potter
Copyeditors: Bridget Reaume, Emmalisa Sparrow Wood
Proofreader: Kristin Thiel
Illustrations: Holly Carton
Design: Sara E. Blum

Manufactured in the United States of America

10 9 8 7 6 5 4 3 2 1

Library of Congress Cataloging-in-Publication Data

Names: Kessler, Lisa (Lisa Anne), author.
Title: The practical tarot method : learn to read tarot cards intuitively /
    Lisa Kessler.
Description: Portland, Oregon : Beyond Words, 2025. | Includes
    bibliographical references.
Identifiers: LCCN 2024036297 (print) | LCCN 2024036298 (ebook) | ISBN
    9781582709413 (paperback) | ISBN 9781582709444 (ebook)
Subjects: LCSH: Tarot.
Classification: LCC BF1879.T2 K49 2025 (print) | LCC BF1879.T2 (ebook) |
    DDC 133.3/2424—dc23/eng/20240903
LC record available at https://lccn.loc.gov/2024036297
LC ebook record available at https://lccn.loc.gov/2024036298

The corporate mission of Beyond Words Publishing, Inc.: *Inspire to Integrity*

FOR KEN

THANKS FOR YOUR UNCONDITIONAL LOVE
AND UNWAVERING SUPPORT.

Contents

Preface ix

Introduction xiii

    What You Will Learn xv

    A Brief History of Tarot xvi

    Tarot 101 xviii

1: Choosing and Using Your Tarot Deck 1

    How to Find the Right Deck for You 2

    Connecting with Your Deck 3

    Working with Themed Decks 5

    What about Oracle Cards? 6

    Intention Is Everything 7

2: Colors and Symbolism in Tarot 11

    Color Meanings 12

    Other Symbolism 15

3: Cycles in Tarot 23

    Cycles from Ace to Ten 25

    Cycles in the Court Cards 31

    Everything Happens for a Reason 34

4: Major Arcana 37

    0: The Fool 38

    1: The Magician 39

    2: The High Priestess 41

    3: The Empress 42

    4: The Emperor 43

    5: The Hierophant 44

    6: The Lovers 46

    7: The Chariot 47

    8: Strength 48

    9: The Hermit 49

10: Wheel of Fortune 50

11: Justice 52

12: The Hanged Man 53

13: Death 54

14: Temperance 55

15: The Devil 57

16: The Tower 58

17: The Star 60

18: The Moon 61

19: The Sun 62

20: Judgement 64

21: The World 65

5: Minor Arcana 67

Cups (Water) 68

Pentacles (Earth) 83

Wands (Fire) 99

Swords (Air) 114

6: Spreads and the Communication Between the Cards 131

One-Card Draw 132

Pulling Multiple Cards for One Question 133

Spreads 135

How to Do a Reading for Another Person 146

7: Practical Uses for Tarot in Everyday Situations 149

Exercises for Daily Practice and Inspiration 150

Tarot Journaling 152

Tarot Meditation 154

Tarot and Manifesting 157

Using Tarot to Inspire Creative Projects 159

Conclusion 163

Acknowledgments 165

Notes 167

About the Author 169

About the Illustrator 171

Preface

There are no coincidences. We've all heard that phrase, but over the years, I've come to accept the truth in it. The Universe is made of energy and we're all a part of it, woven into a galaxy of stars.

This book crossed your path for a reason. Divine timing is at work, and you are right where you are supposed to be.

There's comfort in that inner "knowing," when we feel most connected to our higher self. *The Practical Tarot Method* is meant to help you deepen your confidence and develop more trust in your own intuition. Tarot cards are a powerful tool to help you tap into a higher power—the Universe, Spirit, Source, Creator, or whatever power you look toward for guidance—and shine a light on your spiritual path. My hope is that this book will make learning to read tarot fun and empowering.

I've taught my Practical Tarot method of reading the cards for more than ten years and read for others for nearly twenty. My love of tarot cards is also woven into my novels and developed into courses

for writers and artists to use tarot to help them tap into their creative intuition. It was while I was teaching a group of writers that I realized it was finally time to write this book and design the *Practical Tarot* deck. The deck was inspired by my love for tarot and my yearning for an intuitive tarot deck that reflected our diverse world. I'm thrilled with how it turned out, and I'll be using those cards on our journey through this book. You will find full-color images of the *Practical Tarot* deck in the insert at the back of the book.

Tarot has woven its threads throughout my life for over twenty years. Despite my having been a published fiction author for more than ten of those years, the thought of bridging these two passions never crossed my mind. Truthfully, the idea of writing a nonfiction book terrified me! Perhaps you are feeling a similar apprehension about studying tarot. Change and growth are often uncomfortable, pushing us out of our comfort zones. Growing pains, right?

{3}
The Empress

Page of Wands

As I sat with my uncertainty, contemplating this new project, I turned to my cards for some insight; I pulled The Empress and the Page of Wands.

The Empress calls us to manifest our dreams. She encourages us that the time for growth is now! The Page of Wands asks us to bring youthful joy and child-like energy to the action of learning.

They are the perfect inspiration and guiding light for this new journey. I hope you'll dive into this study with the same enthusiasm too.

This book isn't intended to teach you to become a tarot card reader for others. (Although you certainly could follow that path.) This tarot journey isn't intended to be a lecture either. Consider this book to be a conversation, meant to help tarot become a useful, practical tool to navigate your everyday life and to help you understand your life experiences and see yourself as Spirit sees you without the filter of your ego or self-consciousness. To that end, you'll find meditation and journaling prompts as well as manifesting tips for each card to encourage you to broaden your personal connection to the cards and allow them to provide support and validation as you journey through life and manifest your dreams.

There are no coincidences. This book crossed your path for a reason.

Maybe you've always had an interest in tarot, maybe tarot cards keep showing up in your social media feed, or maybe you're just curious. Either way, I'm eager for you to join me on this journey, and I'm honored to walk this path with you.

Lisa

Introduction

I didn't take to tarot right away. When I purchased my first deck—a traditional Rider-Waite Tarot deck—I was a new mom, and I was seeking the spiritual insight tarot offered. However, I didn't connect with the art on the cards and memorizing all seventy-eight in the deck quickly overwhelmed me. I set it aside and sought out another metaphysical tool that might work for me.

Time passed, yet I kept coming back to tarot and buying new decks. Eventually I found one with artwork that truly resonated with me, and I started to recognize patterns and symbols in the cards across all the decks. I began comparing them and jotting down notes.

This "language" in the cards made learning more intuitive. The process became fun and exciting instead of a stressful memorization exercise. I started to think of my tarot deck like a cell phone I could pick up to reach the Universe when I needed advice or direction. It became part of my life in a practical way. That is what *The Practical Tarot Method* is all about.

This technique of reading the cards intuitively provides an accessible and widely applicable way of using tarot. It's not meant to be a rule book. In fact, because everyone has had different life experiences, there are no hard and fast rules when it comes to your intuition. The card interpretations you will find in this book are subjective. As you work with the cards and form your own personal connections, your intuition will strengthen, and so will the information you receive from your deck.

For centuries, many different cultures have turned to divination decks like tarot and oracle cards to gain clarity with the higher self and the Universal energy around them. Movies and television tend to use tarot as a plot device to tell the future or to add a scary element, perpetuating the idea that the cards themselves are magic and represent chaotic evil at times, but, in reality, tarot cards are simply images printed on card stock with symbols and cycles to represent every aspect of our human experience. They may help you catch a glimpse of insight for the future, but it's your intuition that leads to that clarity. Your cards are just a helpful means to get there.

What You Will Learn

In chapter 1, we'll address how to find the right tarot deck that speaks to your intuition. In chapters 2 through 5, you'll learn about the symbolism, colors, cycles, and traditional meanings of the cards, but as you work with them, you'll cultivate even deeper meanings. This is the magic of tarot.

As you dive into chapters 4 and 5, you'll find the traditional meanings for the individual cards for both the Major and Minor Arcana. Every card includes a descriptive interpretation of its traditional meaning, meditation and journal prompts to strengthen your connection to the card's meaning, manifesting tips, and helpful keywords. Because your intuition is the heart of *The Practical Tarot Method*, I encourage you to think of the keywords as inspiration if you're struggling to interpret a card's meaning in relation to your current life. The keywords are not intended for memorizing or to be the definitive meaning of the card. Nothing about tarot is written in stone; that's why your intuition is such an important part of your interpretation.

You'll also learn about the power of divination spreads in chapter 6, as well as practical ways to infuse tarot into your daily life in chapter 7. There are several exercises sprinkled throughout the book to give you a chance to use your tarot cards in different ways and familiarize yourself with the Practical Tarot method. The more you use the cards, the more your confidence in your higher wisdom and spiritual gifts will expand.

A Brief History of Tarot

The seventy-eight-card tarot decks commonly used today came out of Italy, France, and Germany in the 1400s. In fact, the word *tarot* was inspired by the Italian word "tarocchi."[1]

Divination through the use of cards, or cartomancy, eventually evolved from the fifty-two-card decks we associate with poker, solitaire, and countless other classic games; the addition of the Major Arcana and the Page cards completed the seventy-eight-card deck we use today. *The Game of Tarots* by Antoine Court de Gébelin was published in 1773 and credited with elevating the tarot card readings from a game into a method to gain esoteric wisdom. He even went so far as to hypothesize that tarot was created by the Egyptians, but there's no evidence to support his claim.[2]

As interest in the occult and metaphysics expanded in the eighteenth and nineteenth centuries, women took on an active role in shaping tarot, although their work has, until recently, been overlooked. British spiritualists, such as Pamela Colman Smith, Frieda Harris, and Madeline Montalban, and American mystics like Madame Marcia Champney cultivated the art and symbolism in tarot, giving women a new path to explore their spiritual gifts.[3]

Probably the world's most well-known tarot deck, the Rider-Waite Tarot, was drawn and designed by Pamela Colman Smith in 1909 under the direction of Arthur Edward Waite. Although he is credited with being the deck's designer, she was the artist behind the iconic images.[4]

Tarot blossomed into the mainstream in the United States during the early 1900s. Even renowned psychiatrist Carl Jung was fascinated by tarot cards, referring to tarot in a 1933 lecture as "an intuitive method that has the purpose of understanding the flow of life, possibly even predicting future events, at all events lending itself to the reading of the conditions of the present moment."[5]

Today, tarot is used by people of all backgrounds for guidance and reflection. As spirituality moves into a new digital age, with social media connecting like-minded people across the globe and influencers showcasing their creative passions with broad new audiences, there is a growing interest in tarot worldwide. According to a Pew Research study conducted in 2023, about 41 percent of Americans report they have become more spiritual over their lifetime, while only 24 percent report they have become more religious.[6] With this growth in spirituality, there is increasing interest in more diverse tarot decks like the *Practical Tarot* deck found in the appendix of this book. As more people worldwide seek spiritual inspiration and insight, we should expect to see tarot continue to evolve.

Tarot 101

Before we dive into how use your tarot deck, let's start with some basics. Every tarot deck contains seventy-eight cards, organized into two categories: the Major Arcana and the Minor Arcana.

The Major Arcana cards are numbered from 0 (The Fool) to 21 (The World), and the Minor Arcana cards are split into four suits representing the four elements of Water, Earth, Fire, and Air. The elements are typically symbolized with Cups, Pentacles, Wands, and Swords, respectively. Each suit card is numbered from Ace to Ten with four additional court cards: Page, Knight, Queen, and King.

The seventy-eight cards each represent different aspects of life and events in our lives. When using them for divination purposes, they can confirm your feelings and intuition and shed light on your path forward when you're feeling unsure which way to turn. You'll find black-and-white images of the cards from my *Practical Tarot* deck alongside each of the card descriptions in chapters 4 and 5, and in the back of the book, you'll find all the cards in their full-color glory.

Keep in mind that tarot cards exist to enhance your personal spirituality and spiritual beliefs. When you see the words *Universe*, *Spirit*,

Divine, *Source*, *God*, or *Creator*, they are open to your interpretation of how you view the energy around you, whether it be a god or goddess of any religion or faith that inspires you.

In this book, we'll explore the elements, symbols, and cycles in tarot that resonate no matter which deck you might be using. Once you learn the universal language of the cards, you won't need to memorize any deck's guidebook or other books on the subject. You'll be able to pull a card or draw a spread from any deck and trust your intuition to unveil the messages. Finally, at the end of our journey, you'll discover some additional ways to incorporate tarot into your everyday life.

Tarot is a deeply meaningful device to tap into Spirit, and your higher self, once you're confident in your ability to "read" the cards. The more you use your deck, the more your confidence will grow; eventually you will learn to trust your intuition, and that inner "knowing" will expand.

I hope you're eager for this new adventure. Let's begin . . .

Choosing and Using Your Tarot Deck

Before we start looking at individual card meanings and symbolism, I encourage you to have a tarot deck on hand for the exercises you'll find in later chapters. If you don't yet have a deck of your own, it can be overwhelming to choose a deck when there are so many choices available. In this chapter there are some tips for finding a deck you connect with and how to spiritually cleanse it and attune your deck to your own energy.

How to Find the Right
Deck for You

When I started my tarot journey, I picked up the traditional Rider-Waite Tarot deck, which is often regarded as a beginner deck. However, no matter how often I tried to memorize card meanings when drawing cards, nothing stuck. I couldn't understand the images and how they related to my life. I got frustrated and turned away from trying to read tarot for a couple years, collecting decks for the beautiful artwork instead.

Occasionally I'd take the Rider-Waite deck off the shelf to try again, but I'd pull cards and feel . . . nothing. I didn't realize it then, but *I* wasn't the problem. That deck simply wasn't for me.

I have nothing against the Rider-Waite deck, and it does work for many people, but it's also not right for everyone. We're all different with unique life experiences. For me, the traditional Rider-Waite deck was filled with many cross-looking men, and I couldn't relate to them. You may have experienced the same thing.

Finding a deck that speaks to you cannot be overstated. When you turn cards, the artwork and symbolism and colors should spark your intuition immediately. They should tell you a story with each card flip. You shouldn't need to reach for the book. Each card should carry a message that you relate to, whether it's the artwork, the number of the cycle, or a completely personal connection to an individual, event, or experience from your past.

These intuitive messages are much more important than the cards' traditional meanings. Tarot cards are a device to help you tap into the wisdom of the Universe, not to memorize and regurgitate. The more you use your deck and trust your instincts as you turn cards, the stronger your connection to your higher self will become. Eventually, you can pull cards as a validation of what your intuition is already whispering. Trust your instincts and remember, you *always* get the card you need.

Connecting with Your Deck

Once you've found a deck that really speaks to you, it's important to bond with it. This relationship can begin with a simple dedication ritual. It doesn't have to be intricate or complicated; it just needs to resonate with you. How can you unbox this deck of cards and make it yours?

Here are four ideas to try. When reading over the following ideas, center yourself and recognize what "feels right" to you. Everyone is different, and if you need to modify any of these techniques, they will still work. This is also a good time to be mindful and avoid appropriating spiritual traditions from cultures outside your own.[7] Beyond this, the only mistake is not listening to your inner voice, so use this time to be creative and perhaps consider making your own traditions in your practice.

꩜ Shuffle the new cards and fan them out on your tarot mat. A mat is usually a square made of velvet or felt so that the cards have enough grip to fan out evenly (on a smooth tabletop, the cards can clump together). Light a candle, or a sage bundle if that's part of your cultural tradition and feels right to do so. Run the flame above the new deck while whispering in your head or aloud: "These cards offer me guidance and validation for my highest good."

꩜ Wait until the full moon to unwrap the cards, shuffle, and then put the deck in the windowsill. Ask the moon's energy to cleanse and dedicate the cards.

꩜ Unwrap your deck and shuffle, place a piece of kyanite, or another crystal that you resonate with, on top of the cards with the intention of cleansing and claiming your deck for your highest good. You could also work with singing bowls or bells to cleanse the deck, whatever feels right.

꩜ Place your deck in a dedicated space, circle the deck with salt and leave it in the circle overnight to cleanse the energy, then shuffle and infuse it with your own energy.

As you can see, there are many ways to build your connection with your new deck and infuse it with your energy. Your intention is the magic, not the ritual you choose. Allow your heart to breathe your own meaning into your cards. Do what feels right to you in order to make your deck your own. These are merely suggestions.

Once you feel ownership of your deck, be sure to use it. Pull a card or a spread every day. One-card pulls with the simple intention "What do I need to know today?" or "What should be my focus today?" are great for this exercise.

Each day you will become more familiar with the cards. First allow your intuition to speak the meaning, and then check the guidebook and see how your idea differs with the traditional meaning. Always trust your intuition, above all. If your interpreted meaning doesn't match the traditional meaning, that's okay. The way you resonate with each card is meaningful and valid. You drew that card to receive that message whether or not it matches the book's explanation.

Working with Themed Decks

Tarot decks have inspired artists around the world, and many choose to design decks around a theme. It could be a holiday like Halloween, a beloved movie like *Hocus Pocus*, or even special animals like cats or pandas.

These decks can be fun and inspiring, but if you choose to use them, keep in mind that they're often modified to better suit the theme. For example, a pirate deck might alter the traditional

Minor Arcana suits, changing the pentacles to coins and wands to pistols. They still convey the elements of Earth and Fire, respectively, but by changing the names, it fits the artwork and feel of the deck better.

Occasionally, a themed deck may also swap names for the Major Arcana cards. An example might be a vampire tarot deck changes The Emperor to Dracula and The Empress to Mina. Neither character truly emulates the traditional meaning of the card, but they definitely support the theme of the deck.

In my personal practice with tarot, I enjoy using themed decks for creative projects. They can inspire scenes for books because every card is colored with that creative vision. If you approach these decks with that intention, they can be a powerful connection to your muse.

What about Oracle Cards?

Oracle cards are often sold alongside tarot decks, but they are not the same tool. While tarot decks have seventy-eight cards that consist of the Major and Minor Arcanas, oracle decks have no such constraints. They can have any number of cards, and the decks will follow an endless variety of themes rather than the traditional tarot cycles. Oracle cards often have words printed on each card depicting the meanings, and they cover the gamut of topics from angels to the zodiac and everything in between. This is not to devalue oracle cards—I use them all the time—as they are simply a different device for acquiring guidance from your higher self. So how do you know which type of cards will work best for you? It depends on the insights you're looking for. When I feel disconnected from Spirit, become caught up in a scarcity mindset, or find myself struggling with self-doubt, I usually reach for my tarot cards. There is comfort in the cycles of the Major and Minor Arcanas that mirror our lives. You may not know exactly which area of your life is the cause of the unease, and tarot cards can help to illuminate the situation.

Oracle cards often have a narrower focus, depending on their theme, which can limit the insight you may be looking for. If you find yourself needing validation that you're reading your tarot spread correctly, this is a great time to pull an oracle card and compare its meaning with the tarot spread. Because there are words on each card, occasionally the oracle card can provide more clarity as well.

Intention Is Everything

With a deck in hand, next we need to focus on intention. Intention, as it relates to tarot, is basically your question to the Universe, or to the cards. This is an important asset as you use your tarot cards. What are you looking for? Clarity, support, insight, validation, and direction can all be gained, but only if you have that intention in mind as you pull your card. It can be as simple as "What do I need to know today?" or as detailed as "What do I need to focus on for my job interview tomorrow?"

The intention you set will guide your hand as you draw, and it gives the card meaning. Without a question, you get answers that have no relevance or meaning. Once your intention is set, the number one rule with tarot—possibly the only real rule—is this: You always pull the card you need. Always. I don't pretend to understand how that happens, but after many, many readings for strangers, I can honestly say this rule is true. Sometimes the card hints at something in the near future and may not immediately resonate, but I promise that it will eventually.

However, without a set intention—a question to the Universe—there's no way to know how to apply the card or which aspect of your life the card is related to. The symbolism, cycles, and traditional meanings of the cards are guides to an answer, but if you don't know what you're asking, the advice from Spirit can be muddied, like floating down a river in a rudderless boat. You might have a vague meaning but nothing concrete to relate it to.

Sometimes you might pull a card that is simply a validation or reinforcement of something you're already pursuing or acting on in your life, but if you didn't set an intention when you drew the card, how would you know for sure? Here is a taste from my own card pull today.

I pulled three cards.

Because they're all Minor Arcana cards (more on this later, I promise), I know that these point to aspects of myself and my life right now. But if I drew them without a specific intention, I would have no idea what they relate to.

Ace of Cups is a new love. Of what? If I had not set an intention, then who knows? And the Nine of Wands means I'm almost finished

Ace of Cups   *Nine of Wands*   *Ace of Swords*

with an activity, but again, which one? My dishwasher is *almost* full. I am *nearing the end* of the book I'm reading. I am just about out of dog food. It could mean anything. And the Ace of Swords indicates a new idea. That's very vague if I don't know which area of my life it's referring to. Maybe the two Aces go together, meaning I'm going to love this new idea. You can think yourself in circles when you don't know why you pulled the cards.

If I set my intention, or ask a question, before pulling the cards, they suddenly paint a very specific picture. My intention when I drew these cards was this: "What do I need to know for my work on *The Practical Tarot Method* book?" Now the cards take on a true and specific meaning. Ace of Cups is a new love; I'm going to love writing this book! The Nine of Wands is telling me I'm almost finished with an activity cycle, and I should keep working until it's finished. At the time of my writing this, the *Practical Tarot* deck cards are almost completed. This is a nudge from the Universe to persevere and finish. And the Ace of Swords is a new idea, and as this is my first nonfiction book, the act of writing this book is a brand-new adventure! This simple three-card spread gave me validation of my path ahead and encouragement to see it through to completion. Do you see the importance of setting your intention when you draw? Having a specific question in mind sheds light on the card's meaning and provides clarity to connect the cards you pulled to your current situation. Without intention, it is impossible to understand why your hand was guided to pull those cards. Questions empower the answers.

Now that you've connected with your deck and are confident in the power of your intention when working with the cards, let's build onto that knowledge with color meanings and symbolism in the artwork. This next step will give your intuition even more to work with before we introduce traditional card meanings.

2

Colors and Symbolism in Tarot

Although popular culture tends to show tarot cards as magical, mystical, and sometimes nefarious plot devices, in reality, the opposite is true. Having a tarot deck on your shelf doesn't mean you have a magical oracle that can tell you the future. Tarot is also not a religion. Whatever your religious background, tarot cards are simply a tool to help connect with your intuition, your higher self, and the energy of the Universe around you. The cards encourage us to set our ego aside and receive a clear message from Source, whatever your belief system deems your Creator to be.

That's why recognizing the imagery and symbolism on the cards is so important and incredibly personal. You might connect with something on that card that has nothing to do with the traditional tarot meaning, and that is completely valid. You wouldn't have been guided to pull that card otherwise. This is your intuition speaking to you. Trust it.

For that reason, we are starting with building your intuitive foundation *before* studying the traditional meanings of the cards. Once you understand the symbols and cycles in the cards, you can form connections even if you haven't mastered the traditional meanings. You won't need to memorize anything to receive meaningful messages from your cards.

At the end of this chapter, you are invited to shuffle and draw three cards to practice with this new connection to your intuition. You'll gain valuable, intuition-led insight before we even touch on the traditional meanings of the individual cards.

Color Meanings

Unless you have a themed deck, most individual cards are intentionally crafted with vivid, specific colors. Keep in mind that there are no hard and fast rules, but these general color associations are a tool to connect with your cards visually. Because the cards are a tool to connect you to your higher self and your intuition, practice being present and studying your initial reaction to the color as you turn over the card. Don't try to convince yourself of something else. We all have intuition, but we need to practice trusting it. Ready to dive in?

- **Purple** represents a deity or Source, Divine inspiration. This may point to your Creator, God, or Pure Love in whatever spiritual tradition you recognize. It may also represent your higher self or super-conscience. When you see purple on a card, this idea or action is divinely inspired or divinely authorized. On traditional decks, this concept is often depicted as a large purple hand reaching out from the clouds, representing the idea or action being handed to you directly from Spirit.

- **Red** represents raw, intense emotions. Rage, love, passion, and drama are all associated with the color. On some cards, you might notice someone wearing a red cloak or a splash of red in the sky, symbolizing strong emotions and often cautioning us to think before we act on emotion alone.

- **Green** represents nature and growth. Manifesting and prosperity are also associated with green. Quite literally, money. However, jealousy and envy are often depicted with green as well. The key comes down to recognizing your initial gut feeling as you draw the card. Do you feel peace at the sight of all the green, or do you immediately recall a situation where you felt envious of someone else or compared your achievements to theirs? Your first impression of the green is your answer.

White in the cards usually represents innocence and angelic beings. Your cards may feature a white dove, signifying angelic influence or messages from Spirit. White, gauzy clouds in the artwork can represent the innocence of youth or guardian angels.

Blue is the color of water and symbolizes our deep emotions. It can also signify peace, serenity, and balance. When you see blue water on your cards, it's usually calling you to recognize how your emotions influence your decisions, or it could be asking you to honor your emotions. Blue can also represent sadness and disappointment. Images of an agitated ocean on cards can symbolize churning emotions while a placid lake would indicate calm, peaceful emotions.

Yellow is the color of the sun. It represents power, joy, and good luck. When you turn a card with a big yellow sun, bright sunflowers, or sun rays coming through the clouds, it symbolizes warmth and happiness, good fortune. Imagine the warmth of the sun on your back, soaking through your clothes and into your skin. This powerful energy radiates from the yellow on your cards. Yellow is an optimistic, positive outlook.

Orange is the color of fire, symbolizing action and newfound energy in a project or activity. A splash of orange on your card can represent your drive to complete tasks, spark creativity, or showcase confidence in your abilities.

It's also a nudge from the Universe to get started and make progress. When orange is present, forward motion is in play.

Brown is the color of earth, reminding us to be practical and grounded in the material world. A card with plenty of brown might be telling you to focus on your physical body and finances. It's important to maintain your balance between your spiritual and material being, and brown is a reminder to eat and sleep and exercise to care for your earthly body.

Black represents power and wisdom and authority. If a character on your cards wears a black cape, it usually depicts a mentor or validates power and judgment in a situation.

Pink symbolizes love and friendship but can also nod toward joy and self-esteem. Seeing a pink sky or pink clothing on a card represents joy, friendship, and potentially love.

Other Symbolism

The colors on your cards aren't the only symbolic messages you can draw from your deck. In addition to the suit symbols of Cups, Pentacles (sometimes referred to as coins or disks), Swords, and Wands (sometimes referred to as staves or rods), there are other universal symbols within the artwork on your cards. They can speak to you in tandem with the colors or independently. Again, allow your intuition to be your guide when drawing a card. Whatever you notice first is the heart of your message.

Decks are also influenced by their creators, so it is not unheard of for some of the following symbolism interpretations to vary artist-to-artist; the following is a universal list of common symbols and meanings found across divination cards.

- **Birds** represent messengers from the spirit realm. When you see birds on the cards, they symbolize your angels and spirit guides. It's also important to notice placement: if the bird is sitting on a character's shoulder, it's indicating that your guides and angels are close. Be on high alert for signs from them. If the birds are depicted in the distance, far from the character on the card, this can be a nudge from Spirit to meditate and ask your guides to come closer to gain clarity. It's a call for you to tap in and actively listen.

- **Doves** and **Hawks** are the messengers from the Universe. Doves are signs of peace and the angelic realms, while Hawks are usually messengers, bringing insights from the Universe and loved ones from the other side.

- **Owls** and **Cranes** represent wisdom. If you see one on your card, this can be a reminder to trust your intuition. You are making wise decisions.

- **Butterflies**, **Dragonflies**, and **Swans** all symbolize transformation into a better version of yourself. Often, you'll see these creatures on cards that encourage personal growth and change. Transformation is always welcomed into our lives, but it's rarely an easy process. The presence of any of these animals is gentle reassurance that a positive outcome awaits at the end of this journey.

- **Infinity Symbols** represent limitless potential and eternal aspirations. This symbol, like a figure eight on its side, often appears on cards calling you to connect with Spirit for manifestation or guidance. It encourages you to tap into the unlimited, never-ending energy of the Universe. It can also symbolize deities and the Source of all.

- **Turtles** symbolize long life and ancestral lines. When you notice a turtle on your card, it can be a call to connect with your ancestors or reminisce about them. Your answers may be found in generations past. Depending on your intention when you drew the card, it can also be a validation that your ancestors are near you, guiding you on your path.

- **Scarabs** were used often in the Egyptian funeral rites, and in divination decks they show up as a symbol of protection, rebirth, and reincarnation. When you find the sacred beetle on your cards, you are safe on your journey.

Cats typically represent boundaries and independence. Cats let you know when you can pet them, and once they're finished, they leave. We can learn much from them by setting our own expectations and limits. When you find a cat on your cards, it's time to re-examine your boundaries with yourself and with others.

Cows symbolize abundance and nurturing. When the cow appears on your cards, relax at the notion that you have—or will soon have—all you need. They are a calming and mothering presence. You will be nurtured on your path. **Bulls** also represent abundance and prosperity, but instead of nurturing, they lean toward fertility.

Lions, **Wolves**, and **Dragons** symbolize inner strength. When your cards include any of these regal beasts, you're reminded of your inner power. If you draw the card when you're feeling less than strong, these animals are a nudge from Spirit to feed your inner power and bolster your strength. Seek out those who will empower and encourage you until you're ready to roar again.

The **Stag** appears on our cards as a representation of leadership and pride; be aware that sometimes your pride and ego can blind you from mistakes made or opportunities to grow. When you draw a card with a stag, look within and ask if this is validation of your current leadership or a reminder not to let arrogance and ego lead the way.

Hearts on tarot cards usually symbolize love and compassion. Keep in mind that this is not limited to romantic love—it may be love of a job, of a spiritual path, or of yourself. A heart can also symbolize empathy and kindness.

The **Sky** matters when it comes to your cards. First, the sky represents the element of Air, which symbolizes our thoughts. A blue, cloudless sky on your cards can represent clarity of mind, while a dark, stormy sky can encourage you to free your mind of grudges or anger.

Water is the element that represents our emotions. A calm and placid body of water indicates peaceful and serene emotions, while tumultuous waters, like a waterfall or waves crashing to the shore, indicate tempestuous feelings. These waters encourage you to question your current emotional state and the emotions of those surrounding you.

Fire is the element that represents action. Flames are usually present on cards that call you to act and get things done. Fire can also represent your passion and desire for a project or a person.

❧ **Coins**, **Gold**, and a **Harvest** all represent the element of Earth, which points to your earthly goods and earthly body. When you see any of these items on your cards, your intuition is calling you to focus on your health or money matters, here in the material realm. They can also symbolize financial abundance and charity.

❧ **Flowers** often have traditional meanings. The most common blooms in tarot are **Roses**, representing love, **Sunflowers** for joy and abundance, and **Daffodils** for new beginnings.

❧ **Rainbows** symbolize hope, renewal, and happiness.

There may be certain symbols that represent something to you on a personal level, and those are valid too. For example, my daughter's nickname is Panda, and whenever I notice one on a tarot card, it indicates to me that this message may relate to her. Again, tarot is simply a tool for you to connect with the Universe, including your spirit guides and angels; they know your personal symbols and always put them in front of you to communicate something. Spirit can only work with the memories and personal experiences you have in your head and heart. When Spirit or a loved one from the other side tries to send you a "sign," it often manifests as something special and personally relevant to *you*.

Here's an example of what I mean: even if the guidebook for your deck describes a card featuring a bear as a call to "save up for winter," but when you flip that card and see the bear, it might remind you that your brother loved bears and you feel a nudge from Spirit to call him. This is a valid message for you. Does that make sense? You pulled that card for a reason. Trust your intuition and your first impression.

The tarot guidebooks that often accompany tarot decks offer insight into what inspired the author or artist of the deck. Sometimes those explanations are right on target for your situation, but often the message you receive from the cards is very personal and based on *your* life experience.

Remember, the cards are just a tool. They're not a magical soothsayer or fortune teller. If your intuition connects with the horse on your card, and your mother used to show horses, this could call you to channel her sense of fairness to resolve a situation in your life. That is a valid reading for that card today. Don't talk yourself out of it.

EXERCISE

Shuffle your cards and spread them out face down. Hover your hand over them and set your intention: "What do I need to know right now?"

Draw three cards and turn them over. Using your new understanding of symbolism and colors, what message do you receive using your intuition alone?

Remember, you *always* get the card you need. Always. Trust your gut. Even though you might not know the traditional meaning of the cards you drew just yet, the symbols and colors should translate enough of a feeling for you to receive a meaningful message. Use the tool at hand (the cards) and tap into your higher self for the answers you seek. As you deepen your knowledge of each of the cards and their cycles, the messages will get even clearer.

3

Cycles in Tarot

Once you have mastered the symbolism on the cards, watch for the cycles, or numbers, in the cards. Everything in our lives comes and goes in cycles, and the cards reflect that. This chapter will focus on the Minor Arcana cards and the cycles of all four elements from Ace, representing a new beginning, through Ten, completing the cycle. From there, we'll review the court cards and their unique cycle from Page to King.

Allow yourself the time to get familiar with your cards now, if you haven't already. I recommend organizing them by Major and Minor Arcanas. The Major Arcana cards are usually numbered 0 to 21, are individually named, and are not associated with a suit. Set aside the Major Arcana cards and then organize the remaining cards (the Minor Arcana) by suit (Cups, Pentacles, Wands, and Swords). From here, order each suit from Ace to Ten. Take the time to browse through each stack of cards you just organized. One of the things you might notice is the cycle's ebb and flow from Ace to Ten. The journey from Ace to Ten is never in a straight line. There are choices to make, obstacles to face, and there are cards in each suit that represent joy, struggle, and everything in between. Tarot cards are a powerful reflection of the paths of our lives. When you're working to accomplish a goal or manifest big changes in your life, often you take five steps ahead and the next day you slide back three. This is the rhythm of life, and tarot follows those natural cycles.

Even the Major Arcana, which we study in depth in chapter four, has a natural cycle from The Fool at the beginning of the twenty-two-card journey to The World at the completion of the progression. The Major Arcana has a longer series than the Minor Arcana, from card 0 to card 21. If you're familiar with the concept of the hero's journey from Joseph Campbell,[8] the Major Arcana cycle is very similar. We start at the "call to adventure," or The Fool, and conclude with The World, a new sense of self or return home to a changed world.[9]

Since tarot cards offer a means to tap into your intuition, memorizing card meanings is far less important than connecting to what your higher self and the Universe are trying to convey. Rather than memorizing every word of the guidebook, it's helpful to focus on where the card falls in the cycle in each suit. In this book and the *Practical Tarot* deck, I've arranged the Minor Arcana with Cups and Pentacles first because their cycles are very similar, with Cups focusing on an emotional journey (Water) and Pentacles concentrating on your material world (Earth). Wands (Fire) and Swords (Air) are then paired because their cycles both end with a burden. If you begin to recognize this pattern, the cycle makes more sense.

Cycles from Ace to Ten

Aces, regardless of suit, always represent new cycles in relation to an aspect of your life, the Twos involve making a choice or choosing, and the Three of Cups and Pentacles both focus on working together with others, whereas the Three in Wands and Swords focus on the individual instead of a group. The Fours and Fives deal with lower vibration emotions, and the Sixes and Sevens break through to hope and possibility. The Eights and Nines involve mastery and efforts paying off. The Ten of both Cups and Pentacles represent the completion of the cycle of love and abundance, while the Ten of the Swords and Wands suits don't end as happily, typically representing a burden. The cycles follow the natural flow of life, with ups and downs that lead to growth.

Here's an example of the flow through Wands if you were looking for a new job or asking about your current job:

- **Ace:** You decide on a new career and have a burst of inspiration to build a new resume and begin your search.

- **Two:** You've interviewed for a variety of positions, and now there are two or more potential paths before you. You need to reflect and make a choice.

- **Three:** You've made your choice, and it's time to take action by joining the company and learning all the new responsibilities that go with it.

- **Four:** You realize you're going to excel at this new endeavor, and your confidence grows. You take on more responsibility and offer more new ideas for growth.

- **Five:** Your ideas are met with a little resistance that cause you to feel like you're battling your teammates. This is when you remember the ultimate goal and work to get everyone on your team headed in the same direction. Compromise is usually necessary.

- **Six:** With the conflict resolved, you receive outward recognition of your accomplishments. You could expect a great review, an award, or a raise.

Seven: Now that your skills have been noticed, perhaps you are given a promotion, but you're still covering your previous responsibilities too. This leaves you feeling alone and struggling to keep up. If you voice your concerns, you could get some assistance.

Eight: Now you're probably tired. You know what needs to be done, and it's time to take action, but you may be making excuses instead. Think of this as a warning about procrastination and get busy again.

Nine: With a renewed sense of purpose, you dive back into the project, filled with inspiration to see it completed.

Ten: As is common when the end is in sight, you may have taken on too much. This card shows the burden you're attempting to carry all on your own. It's time to stop trying to do everything. Focus on one task at a time and ask for help if you need it.

The cycle chart on the following pages can help you see the similarities between each of the suits and elements depending on where the card falls in the cycles. See if you can feel the natural rhythm of each cycle as it moves through each aspect your life.

MINOR ARCANA CYCLES

Card Number within the Suits	CUPS (Water—Emotions)	PENTACLES (Earth—Earthly Goods & Physical Health)
Ace	A new cycle of love begins.	A new material cycle of money or health begins.
Two	It's time to choose a partner with your heart.	It's time to choose a job or health goal or find balance in your life.
Three	It's time to celebrate the love of friends.	It's time to network with friends to prosper financially or physically.
Four	You're envying what your friends have.	You're clinging to money or material possessions too tightly. You might be too controlling with your new diet or exercise program.
Five	You're feeling grief or loss—but it only hurts because the love was real.	You're feeling left out of an opportunity, but you can still knock on that door.
Six	Nostalgia; you're remembering the past with rose-colored glasses.	Charity; you have enough to give back to others.
Seven	You can manifest anything. Choose your next dream with your heart. What would bring you joy?	Your efforts are about to pay off. It's almost time to harvest what you've planted.

WANDS (Fire—Actions & Projects)	SWORDS (Air—Thoughts)
A new cycle of activity or a project starts.	A new cycle of thought or idea begins.
It's time to choose which project to pursue.	It's time to make a decision, but you're resisting the choice.
You've made your decision on a project; now it's time to take action.	You've hit an obstacle but may be exaggerating the outcome in your head.
You're starting to gain confidence in your abilities and a new project.	After the drama, it's time to rest and clear your head.
The project is getting chaotic— your teammates may need redirection to work together.	You're feeling anxious, worried what others might be thinking.
Sweet victory; you may expect outward recognition, accolades, or awards for your excellence at your activity.	You may be headed down a path others think will be best for you. Grab the rudder and sail your own ship.
You're taking on all the work alone. Working overtime. Ask for help.	Paranoia; you're worried that someone might be doing something to hurt you and are gathering swords for a battle that may be only in your head.

(continued on following page)

Card Number within the Suits	CUPS (Water—Emotions)	PENTACLES (Earth—Earthly Goods & Physical Health)
Eight	It's time for a new journey of love.	You're saving money and moving from apprentice to master. A promotion at work is near.
Nine	Make a wish. All the dreams of your heart are close by, or this could be validation that a piece is missing in this relationship. Trust your intuition.	It's time to enjoy the fruits of your labor. Treat yourself a little— you've earned it.
Ten	You've completed a cycle of love. Celebrate your happily ever after.	You've completed a cycle of health and money. Abundance surrounds you.

Do you see how the Minor Arcana reflects the cycles in our lives? Once you internalize this natural progression from Ace to Ten, you can read the cards without any memorization. This practice also makes each message more personal to you as you flip the cards over.

WANDS (Fire—Actions & Projects)	SWORDS (Air—Thoughts)
You know what needs to be done to complete your project, but you are also tired. Procrastination might be setting in.	You feel trapped in a situation, but you are the one holding the blindfold. Take a deep breath and look at the situation again. You will see the solution.
You are ready for the final push across the finish line of your project. Take action.	Your worries hang over you, causing you to lose sleep. Insomnia might be plaguing you. Meditate and release your fears.
You may have taken on too much all at once. Your project has become a burden.	You may feel like nothing is going right and there is no path forward, but lift your head. There is a new day full of blessings on the horizon.

Cycles in the Court Cards

You may have noticed that the chart didn't include the court cards. The Page, Knight, Queen, and King have their own cycles and energies through our lifespans. The Page is youthful innocence, your inner child. The Knight represents that frenetic, impulsive energy of teens and early adulthood. The Queen and King represent adulthood, but the Queen is the maternal energy to care for others in your circle, and the King represents the more paternal need to lead and protect those in your care.

Occasionally the court cards are more literal and represent a person in your life. If you turn over a King card and immediately your father pops in your head, then the message is representative of him, this time.

COURT CARD CYCLES

Court Card within the Suits	CUPS (Water—Emotions)	PENTACLES (Earth—Earthly Goods & Physical Health)
Page	What did you love as a child? How can you incorporate that love into this situation?	How did you imagine you would make money when you grew up? What did you imagine you would do as an adult? How can you fit some of those aspects into your current material world?
Knight	You could be rushing into a new relationship or opportunity. Be sure you know what you want before infatuation sweeps you up.	Research investments, health products, and job opportunities before diving in. If it seems too good to be true, it often is.

Instead of reflecting cycles of life, the court cards usually represent your mindset. They can also be modifiers for the card spread you've pulled. Perhaps you've pulled a few cards for starting your own business and mixed in with the Wands, you also draw a Page. This card reminds you to keep it fun. Find a way to honor your inner child and the pressure and stress will lift because you'll also enjoy it.

WANDS (Fire—Actions & Projects)	SWORDS (Air—Thoughts)
What did you enjoy doing when you were younger? Can you incorporate some of those activities into your current projects?	What ideas captivated you when you were younger? Can you infuse your current situation with some of these? Allow the innocence to permeate any mental blocks to find new solutions.
You're passionate about your new project and eager to get started. Be sure to pause and make a plan to be sure you can see it through to completion.	A great idea has crossed your path. It's divinely inspired, but take the time to think it through before you take action so you can bring it into reality.

(continued on following page)

Court Card within the Suits	CUPS (Water—Emotions)	PENTACLES (Earth—Earthly Goods & Physical Health)
Queen	You are very intuitive and empathic, but be alert that these gifts don't cause you to become emotionally manipulative. Love is not a possession to put on a shelf, you must participate in the relationship to keep it blooming.	You are a healer with a heart for nurturing others. Abundance is all around you, and you share with those in your care. Be sure that you save some of that healing for yourself. Spreading yourself too thin can lead to burnout if you get too caught up in materialism.
King	You have a big heart and care deeply for others, but this honorable trait may have led to pain in the past. Don't let heartbreak lead to being emotionally withdrawn. Get back into the watery emotions and keep your heart open.	Abundance is all around you, and you take care of those around you. Remember to balance the material world with the spiritual to avoid being greedy. Money is not the answer to every obstacle.

Everything Happens for a Reason

As I mentioned at the beginning of this book, you always get the card you need. However, you might occasionally pull a card from a suit that you don't expect. For example, perhaps you ask a question about moving to a different department at your job, and mixed in with the Wands and Pentacles, you also pull the Three of Cups.

WANDS
(Fire—Actions & Projects)

SWORDS
(Air—Thoughts)

Have you been too busy doing things for others that you have no time for your own projects? Practice healthy boundaries. Just because you can do everything for everyone doesn't mean you should.

You are an excellent communicator and logical thinker; however, this can leave you living in your head too often. Be sure to add empathy to your clear advice.

You are protective of those you care about and a natural leader. Your fearless nature may lead you to be impatient with others at times. Temper your fire with compassion.

Intelligence and rational thinking are your strong suits. You are wise and grounded in your thinking, but your advice can come off as cold and manipulative at times. Tap into your heart and allow others' opinions to be heard.

Three of Cups

This card combination could indicate that you'll make new friends in the new department. It could advise that you should maintain and nurture the friendships you made in your previous department. Celebrate your role change with them. Trust your first thought when you turn the card—that's your intuition in its purest form. You pulled the card for a reason; it's part of the message even if it's not the answer you were expecting.

EXERCISE

Shuffle all of the Minor Arcana cards together now and spread them out face down. Hover your hand over them and set your intention. For this practice, let's use the intention of "What is my focus for this week?"

Draw three cards and turn them over. Using your combined understanding of symbolism, colors, and now cycles as well, see if you can get a clear message using your intuition alone.

Feel free to keep the Minor Arcana cards together and continue practicing with them. Trust your intuition and try to connect with the message of the cards without reaching for the traditional meanings that follow in the next chapter. Once you feel comfortable with the cycles, we'll look at the traditional card meanings in the next two chapters, starting with the Major Arcana cards 0–21.

4

The Major Arcana

The Major Arcana cards are a numbered cycle like the Minor Arcana, but these cards tend to focus on events in our lives and opportunities entering our days, as well as guidance and validation for situations we may already be facing. Instead of a ten-card cycle like the Minor Arcana, the Major Arcana has twenty-two cards from card 0, The Fool, to card 21, The World.

The Fool is the beginning of a new quest or cycle, and you journey through the highs and lows of life, from finding a mentor and experiencing success, to closing chapters, releasing what no longer serves you, finding your new calling, and transforming into a new sense of self. You can find all of the cards in full color in the back of the book.

To deepen your connection with the cards, I've included some suggested topics to journal or meditate on the meanings, as well as some manifesting tips and the correlating zodiac/astrological connection. These associations with the zodiac signs and celestial bodies or planets can help you gain insight into the energy of each card and create another avenue to connect without memorizing specific meanings. These exercises will give you a more personal connection to each card as well as inspiration to manifest positive change.

You're doing a great job so far. Ready for more?

Let's explore the Major Arcana.

{0}

The Fool

The Fool is calling on you to take a leap of faith and believe in yourself. A new opportunity is entering your life, and although it may be out of your comfort zone, drawing The Fool does *not* mean you are going to look foolish. Trust yourself and take the risk. This is an opportunity to learn and grow, a chance to spread wings you never realized you had.

A bright sunrise is on the horizon, and the daffodils at her feet represent a fresh beginning. She looks to the heavens, trusting the Universe as she takes a leap of faith in the direction of her dreams.

Journal or Meditate: In what area of my life do I need to take more risks?

Keywords: New beginnings, adventure, potential, spontaneity, leap of faith, risk-taking, freedom

Manifesting Tip: This is the time to say yes to opportunities and take a few risks. Your dreams are just outside of your comfort zone. Stretch yourself and welcome new adventures as your manifesting journey begins or takes a new direction.

Zodiac/Astrology Connection: Uranus—the seventh planet from the sun—represents innovation and individuality. This sense of awakening and transformation speaks to the energy of The Fool's willingness to try something new.

{1}
The Magician

{1}

The Magician

The Magician represents the ability to reach into the Universe, pluck out your dreams, and bring them into reality. You will manifest something so quickly that it will seem like magic. This is the time to be creative, decide what you want, and go after it. You have all the tools and elements within your reach and your connection to Spirit is strong, but you must firmly decide what you want. Your needs will be met once you identify what you desire.

The infinite possibilities of the Universe are at her fingertips as she reaches one hand into infinity. Her other hand remains grounded on her ritual table, representing the balance between the spiritual and material worlds.

Journal or Meditate: What do I yearn to bring into my life right now?

Keywords: Manifestation, focus, creation, resourcefulness, communication, confidence

Manifesting Tip: Your energy is in tune with the Universe to manifest something new. This alignment allows your intention to quickly manifest into reality. A clear vision of your goal is important. Clarity and creativity are key at this time.

Zodiac/Astrology Connection: Mercury—this planet was named after the messenger of the gods, noted for his speed and swiftness. Mercury embodies immediacy as well as adaptability and reasoning, all beneficial qualities when bringing dreams into reality.

{2}
The High Priestess

The High Priestess is calling you to reconnect with the pure energy of Spirit. Meditate, journal, pray, and remember that you are part of the vast tapestry of stars in the cosmos. Open yourself to the profound wisdom of the Universe and trust your intuition. Watch for signs and follow them for more enlightenment. This is a time to strengthen your metaphysical gifts.

With her third eye open to the mysteries of the spiritual world, welcoming the wisdom of the Divine into her consciousness. In her hands she cradles the Akashic records and her crystal scrying ball.

Journal or Meditate: How can I deepen my connection with the Divine?

Keywords: Divination, knowledge, actualization, intuition, instinct, mystery

Manifesting Tip: The High Priestess encourages you to trust your intuition and the Universe. Meditate on your goals and tap into the wisdom of your spirit guides and angels to inspire you in cocreating your best life path. They can also help you sift through your illusions and fears to find your true current reality.

{2}

The High Priestess

Zodiac/Astrology Connection: The Moon—the moon is a dreamy, watery celestial body calling to the Divine feminine of the priestess. It's associated with dreams, intuition, and habits.

{3}
The Empress

The Empress represents the long-term manifestation of big dreams and goals. This is also a time to give birth to new creative ideas. Take daily steps toward actualizing the new life you crave. You are worthy of the abundance entering your world as you cocreate your reality with Spirit. Now is the time to grow and expand. Depending on your intention, this card can also represent a pregnancy or fertility.

She wears a crown of twelve stars signifying the twelve months of the year. Her pregnant belly is ready to birth new dreams into the world. She wears a green dress—the color of manifestation—and holds wheat in her hand, representing the ability to grow and provide what she needs.

{3}
The Empress

Journal or Meditate: What am I ready to manifest into my life this year?

Keywords: Growth, creation, nurture, abundance, birth, compassion, fertility, motherhood

Manifesting Tip: Begin manifesting a long-term dream. This card signifies a gestating idea or a goal ready to bring it to fruition. Unlike The Magician, the dream indicated by The Empress is usually larger and broader, perhaps encompassing many smaller goals along the path. Your creativity is heightened, so dream big when The Empress crosses your path.

Zodiac/Astrology Connection: Venus—this planet was named after the goddess of love and fertility. It's associated with the color green, symbolizing manifesting, fertility, and creativity.

{4}
The Emperor

The Emperor represents divine masculine energy. You are being called to make your world a better place. This card symbolizes authority, judgment, and compassionate leadership. Tap into your ambition with confidence. The world is yours. Care for those in your life who need your guidance or comfort. Be the leader you are destined to be.

His throne is the world itself, but he is not a tyrant or a bully lording over it. There is affection in his smile. The birds represent his connection to his spirit guides and angels. He is an intuitive leader.

{4}
The Emperor

Journal or Meditate: Where can I take more of a leadership role in my life?

Keywords: Authority, reason, logic, stability, strategy, discipline, responsibility

Manifesting Tip: Right now, your dreams will be better served by leaning into your Divine Masculine energy, which means being structured and disciplined in your actions and not allowing your emotions to take charge. Choose intellect and care for others as you navigate your path forward.

Zodiac/Astrology Connection: Aries—Aries is often a headstrong warrior willing to fight for what they want. Be aware that this passionate Fire sign can sometimes produce stubbornness.

{5}

The Hierophant

The Hierophant is calling on you to expand your knowledge, to learn and grow. Find a mentor or become a mentor for someone else. These lessons can also be spiritual. Make room and time in your life for wisdom and growth. Take a class or join a group. Now is the time to be a seeker or a teacher. You choose.

Surrounded by their books, they beckon you forward with their right hand. In their left, they hold the keys to knowledge and enlightenment. Behind them is a globe representing the world of knowledge available to you.

Journal or Meditate: Where can I expand or share my wisdom and knowledge?

Keywords: Tradition, teacher, spiritual guidance, structure, convention

Manifesting Tip: Expand your knowledge and share it with others. The connections you make through mentoring or being mentored will lead you to new opportunities, and the lessons learned will aid you in bringing your dreams to fruition.

Zodiac/Astrology Connection: Taurus—this Earth sign reflects the practical, slow-and-steady progress toward your dreams. Each step on your journey has meaning and brings your vision closer to reality. Taurus is reliable and a wise reflection of The Hierophant's energy.

{5}

The Hierophant

{6}
The Lovers

The Lovers is about making a conscious choice to partner with someone for a common cause. This is a good time to cultivate meaningful partnerships built on equal footing. Whether a romantic or business partnership, your shared vision will lead to success. Establishing and nurturing healthy boundaries will be important as you forge this alliance to build a brighter future.

The flags snap in the breeze against a blue sky, representing a bright new day. Two female knights have come together, unified in their partnership to win the games. They each have different strengths and backgrounds, but their commitment to their ultimate goal will lead to victory.

{6}
The Lovers

Journal or Meditate: Where would a partnership benefit me in my life right now?

Keywords: Unity, partnership, guidance, devotion, passion, cooperation

Manifesting Tip: Look for a chance for partnership opportunities. When both parties strive for a common goal, success is assured. Finding the right person to help you reach your dreams will make all the difference, but it will also require clear communication and thoughtful planning.

Zodiac/Astrology Connection: Gemini—this Air sign symbolizes two halves of a greater whole. Intellect and logic rule. Seeing and understanding both sides of a situation is required before making life decisions.

{7}

The Chariot

It's time to move forward and take action. The Chariot represents movement in your life. This may be a physical move, like a new house or apartment or a new job, and sometimes it's metaphorical, like acting on a new plan you've been contemplating. Watch for signs from Spirit to guide you on this new journey. You are being led toward a fresh opportunity. Victory is yours.

Her horses are white and black, yin and yang, symbolizing her duality and balance. She unites light and shadow to move to her next dream with conviction. Her spirit guides soar close by, guiding her, and her excitement is obvious as she embraces the changes coming into her life.

Journal or Meditate: Where do I want to go next in my life?

Keywords: Victory, energy, movement, courage, guidance, balance, drive, grit, determination

The Chariot

Manifesting Tip: Move toward your dream. No more waiting. Trust your intuition to guide you down your path. The black and white horses represent the emotional balance you need as you overcome obstacles to reach the victory of dreams made real.

Zodiac/Astrology Connection: Cancer—this Water sign depends on strong intuition in tandem with determination and drive to achieve their objective. While emotions run deep within Cancers, they are also inspired by the moon and its rhythm, keeping a steady pace.

{8}

Strength

{8}

Strength

It's time to feed your inner lion. Spend time with people who empower you. Do activities that fire you up and make you feel strong. Be brave and shine your light into the world, but while you tap into your inner strength and desires, balance it with compassion. True strength is never being a bully; it's shown in caring for those who need protection. You will be an inspiration to others.

The fire of determination burns in her eyes as her soul rises like a phoenix. Her inner lions flank her while she cradles a lamb in her arms. She is strong, but caring, and ready to persevere and overcome any challenges.

Journal or Meditate: How can I feed my inner lion and bolster my determination?

Keywords: Courage, fortitude, compassion, vitality, self-awareness

Manifesting Tip: Feed your inner lion and keep your regal head high as you pursue your big dreams. You have the bravery and fortitude to climb any mountain that comes between you and your goal. Focus on empowerment. There is no room for doubt.

Zodiac/Astrology Connection: Leo—this regal Fire sign has the courageous heart of a lion with compassion and a deep desire to protect others. Confidence and strong leadership add to a Leo's strength.

{9}

The Hermit

{9}

The Hermit

The Hermit is a call to shine a light within. The answers you seek are already inside you. Make time to meditate or journal and tap into your higher self. Consider exploring self-help books or podcasts for deeper enlightenment. The Universe offers wisdom and guidance when you connect with Source energy. Take a moment to breathe and step back from the chaos of life. This is a time for inner reflection.

He sits alone in his cavern with his crystals, reflecting their light within. The purple glow represents divine enlightenment, and the toadstools that grow on and around him symbolize his spiritual transformation.

Journal or Meditate: What have I already been taught but have not learned? How can I unlock more of my authentic self?

Keywords: Wisdom, scholarship, solitude, enlightenment, introspection, contemplation, illumination

Manifesting Tip: You may have encountered an obstacle that has you questioning everything. Now is the time for some solitude to find the answers you seek. Although it may seem as though your progress has slowed, this pause will bring with it new clarity.

Zodiac/Astrology Connection: Virgo—this analytical Earth sign is a master at problem-solving. Valuable insights will be discovered if given the quiet time for a methodical study of the situation.

{10}
Wheel of Fortune

You have reached a crossroads, a turning point, and you need to choose. Which direction will you go? Welcome this fork in the road. Trust your intuition as you make your choice. Luck is on your side.

Follow the signs to your destiny, but remember that you have free-will, so you choose your path forward. Fate has brought you to this crossroads. This is not a time to hesitate.

She meditates on the wheel of fortune, contemplating her next move. With the lion representing her inner strength, the bull symbolizing abundance, and the parrot signifying her spirit guides and angels, she cannot make a wrong choice. Success is just down the road.

Journal or Meditate: What have been the crossroads in my life and the choices I've made? Which path will I choose now?

Keywords: Fate, destiny, change, turning point, serendipity, possibility, expansion, movement

Manifesting Tip: There are so many paths to choose; commit to a direction. Luck is on your side no matter which way you go. Making a choice and continuing your progress is important in this moment. Enjoy the journey. You cannot make a bad decision right now.

Zodiac/Astrology Connection: Jupiter—Jupiter is the fourth-brightest planet and represents growth, prosperity, and expansion. The urge for exploration and willingness to gamble are also strong.

{10}

Wheel of Fortune

{11}
Justice

This is often referred to as the karma card because your actions are being weighed. Often a decision is being made and you have no control over the outcome. Pulling this card means the conclusion will be for your highest good, even if it's not what you currently want. This can refer to legal matters, being hired for a new job, or even being accepted into a college program.

She holds the scale in her right hand, representing wisdom and truth, and the sword in her left, representing the element of Air and clear communication. The glow of divine light behind her head reminds you that Spirit is in control.

{11}
Justice

Journal or Meditate: What past decisions had a lasting effect on me? Did the final outcomes of those decisions lead to growth?

Keywords: Fairness, balance, justice, righteousness, equity, grace, harmony, truth

Manifesting Tip: Trust that the outcomes and decisions unfolding before you are guiding you closer to your goal. This isn't a time for anxiety or indecision. Look at the situation from both sides with a clear head and have faith in the answers you receive.

Zodiac/Astrology Connection: Libra—this Air sign is a great peacemaker, able to see conflicts from both sides and find a balanced solution. A karmic equilibrium is unfolding.

{12}

The Hanged Man

The Hanged Man represents changing your point of view and looking at a situation from a whole new angle. This new perspective may bring enlightenment and peace. It's safe to surrender to the divine flow and try something new. This may seem like a sacrifice, but it will lead to growth. Say yes to something you might normally avoid. Walk an unfamiliar path.

They see the world from a new angle, with the water below representing emotions like fear and curiosity, while the bird on the rope above symbolizes their spirit guides and guardian angels holding them up. The raven on their shirt signifies the messenger from Spirit bringing new wisdom and enlightenment.

Journal or Mediate: How can I approach a current problem from a different perspective right now? What can I say yes to?

Keywords: Tranquility, divinity, patience, self-sacrifice, perspective, self-reliance

Manifesting Tip: Are you beginning to see cycles repeating themselves when it comes to your manifesting journey? Try looking at the issue from a completely different angle. This fresh point of view will allow you to respond in a new way, and the path forward will be discovered. Be willing to sacrifice old beliefs and accept this new perspective.

Zodiac/Astrology Connection: Neptune—the blue planet is associated with dreams and fantasies, including the murky realms of the subconscious. Welcome the fluid nature of the watery planet to dissolve preconceptions.

{13}
Death

{13}
Death

The Death card recognizes the cycles in life. This is a call to close a chapter so that you can open a new one. It is time to finish the situation, and then begin again. It is fine to mourn the ending of one cycle as you celebrate the birth of another. This is a card of transformation and fresh starts. Be willing to shed the old, stagnant reality and step into a fresh cycle of growth.

She surrenders to the colorless ending of a cycle, surrounded by cypress and stinging nettle, signifying mourning, as her spirit moves into a bright spring full of promise. Her violet dress represents her connection to spirit, and her new path is lined with daffodils symbolizing new beginnings and oak trees representing her strength.

Journal or Meditate: What is coming to an end in my life? What new cycle is beginning?

Keywords: Ending, transformation, rebirth, cycles, change

Manifesting Tip: There is no finish line when you're manifesting. Completing one dream opens the door to a new opportunity, and the cycle continues. Finish up your current projects and commitments and step into the bright future that awaits you. You cannot begin anew without letting go of the past.

Zodiac/Astrology Connection: Scorpio—this Water sign dives deep into intense emotions and hungers for transformation. Scorpios are eager to break away from attachments and ascend to the next mystery. Following their intuition, they evolve into a new sense of self easily.

{14}
Temperance

This is a time for patience and balance. Be mindful to eat, drink, sleep, and exercise; nourishing your body will support every other area of your life. Focus on your personal equilibrium while you pause before moving forward. Try to fill your cups evenly. This practice will bring you peace of both mind and body while preparing you for the next step of your journey.

She is surrounded by water, symbolizing abundant emotions. While she concentrates on pouring equal amounts of water into each cup, her focus calms her thoughts and feelings, preparing her to take action in the future.

Journal or Meditate: Where am I out of balance right now?

Keywords: Balance, moderation, stasis between material and spiritual, emotion versus rationality

Manifesting Tip: Find your balance. You may be so eager to see your dream manifested that you're making sacrifices in other areas of your life. Slow down and regain your equilibrium. Everything will unfold according to Divine timing. Forcing it will not bring about the changes you're hoping for.

Zodiac/Astrology Connection: Sagittarius—this Fire sign is an optimistic freedom seeker who sometimes spreads themselves too thin. Temperance in all things will keep Sagittarians from burning out.

{15}
The Devil

This card calls you to examine your life and where you are expending your energy. It's time to give up what no longer serves you. This can represent addictions, self-destructive behavior like greed or envy (as represented by the green background), or relationships that drain your energy, giving nothing in return. Release yourself from the bonds of poisonous cycles in your life so that you can step into the future healthy and whole.

In his greed as he forages through the garden, The Devil has scooped up poison ivy, oleander, deadly nightshade, and toadstools, so while his arms are full, the bounty is toxic. He kneels in poison ivy, and his eyes are already red and itchy, but he still won't abandon his treasure.

Journal or Meditate: Where are my efforts and energy going? What is no longer serving my highest good?

Keywords: Vice, temptation, will, materialism, attachment, desire, restriction

Manifesting Tip: Is your dream serving you, or are you serving it? Take another look at your reasons for pursuing this goal. Will it bring joy and fulfillment? Meditate on these ideas and recognize that

{15}
The Devil

sometimes you need to unchain yourself from old dreams that no longer bring you joy or raise your vibration.

Zodiac/Astrology Connection: Capricorn—this Earth sign is an ambitious leader with a tendency to sacrifice too much in order to reach their goal. In an effort to strive for more, they sometimes find themselves in toxic situations. It's time to break the cycle and reclaim your power.

{16}
The Tower

{16}
The Tower

The Tower represents a major change coming into your life. While sudden unexpected shifts may feel uncomfortable, this is where transformation begins. Perhaps the tower you are enclosed in is actually a chrysalis, and when the chaos settles, you will emerge as a butterfly, enlightened with new wings. The pandemonium of change can be uncomfortable, but you are stronger than you know. This is a chance to expand, grow, and strengthen your foundation. This card calls you to be aware—not afraid—of the change that is on the horizon.

As the lightning strikes around her, she will emerge from the ruins as a new being of light with a resilience and beauty that can only come from weathering a storm. She will rebuild with confidence. Her transformation has given her wings.

Journal or Meditate: What are past changes that I never saw coming? How did they impact my future? How will new, impending changes help me grow?

Keywords: Change, disruption, transformation, reassessment, renovation, obstacles, loss

Manifesting Tip: Be prepared for some epic unplanned events on the way to your dream. Try to be flexible and understand that with change also comes growth. Often The Tower clears the way for bigger and better things that you hadn't even imagined before.

Zodiac/Astrology Connection: Mars—the red planet, associated with the god of war, represents action, aggression, and energy. It can feel like you're in a battle when The Tower brings abrupt changes into your life.

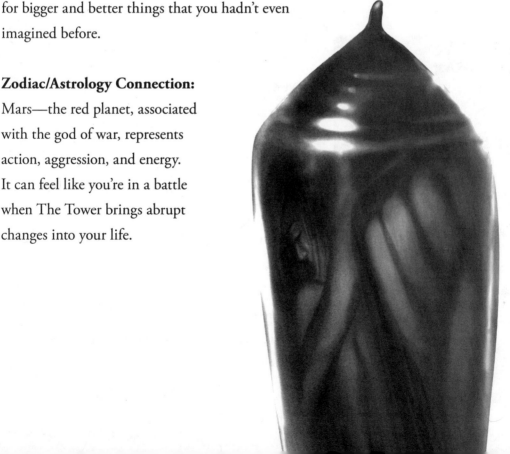

{17}

The Star

The Star offers us hope and guidance. This card can signal a call to map out a path to your new dream. How will you reach your star? Trust your intuition and watch for signs as you plot your course to a brighter future. You are on your path to success. This card can also represent a light in the darkness. You may be that hope for someone who is in desperate need of light. Offer help where it's needed.

She sits under the galaxy of stars with a blank canvas, ready to map her way to her next dream. The yellow of her dress represents her creativity and optimism. The stars are aligned for her highest good.

Journal or Meditate: What small steps can I take on the path to my dream this week?

Keywords: Hope, love, health, reflection, healing, blessings, renewal, recovery

Manifesting Tip: Tap into your intuition as you plot your course to your big dream. Hope for the future will be your light as you continue this journey. Look for goals that can also have a positive impact on others around you.

Zodiac/Astrology Connection: Aquarius— Aquarians are often innovative thinkers with humanitarian hearts that shine their light to be a force for positive change in the world. This Air sign can be eccentric and unconventional at times.

{18}
The Moon

Dream big dreams, but pause here before taking action. Everything looks beautiful in the moonlight. It is not always clear what is real and what is an illusion. This is a great card for brainstorming your next big dream, then meditating on it before you start making concrete plans. Allow your intuition to show you the path forward. Be aware that sometimes fear shrouds what lies ahead, so be prepared to push through. Your dreams are worth the effort.

She sits in an upside-down dream where a wolf is in the water and the fish glide through the air. Her feet dip into the watery world of possibility as she allows herself to imagine without limits.

Journal or Meditate: If anything was possible, what would I bring into my limitless world?

Keywords: Insight, intuition, power, creativity, subconscious, introspection, dreams

Manifesting Tip: When it comes to manifesting your dream, lean into intuition over rationality. Have you been experiencing lucid dreams? Write them down. Make lists of potential goals. Meditate and sail into the murky waters of the subconscious to discover the secret dreams you may have hidden there.

Zodiac/Astrology Connection: Pisces—this Water sign is an intuitive dreamer. Their creativity is inspired from within. Inner knowing and spirituality is their compass in all things.

{19}

The Sun

Inspiration, luck, and success are yours. This card is telling you to say yes to abundance and fulfillment. They are yours. The energy of the sun stimulates renewed positivity and offers you the passion to dive into projects and inspire others. Your enthusiasm is contagious as all of your hard work begins to pay off.

She is draped in wisteria, which represents abundance, and sunflowers, which represent joy and adoration. The yellow and gold of the sun symbolize happiness, bliss, and power. The sun is shining on her back, radiating with life and vitality, and filling her with pure inspiration.

Journal or Meditate: What can I do today to bring more joy into my life?

Keywords: Achievement, success, illumination, confidence, knowledge, vitality, creativity

Manifesting Tip: Your dream is right around the corner. Keep your vibration lifted into joy and gratitude to attract more of the same. Dancing will also lift your energy. Get outside in nature and allow the sun to warm your back. This card validates that you're on the right track.

Zodiac/Astrology Connection: Sun—the fiery star at the center of our galaxy makes life on this planet possible. It is our power source and represents vitality and pride as all the planets orbit around it.

{20}

Judgement

This card is about finding your true calling or purpose. Your spiritual awakening is at hand. All the triumphs and trials of your life have been preparing you for this new cycle of growth. You are inspired and driven now that you see your genuine spiritual reflection. Accept your full potential and walk your enlightened path.

The angel blows his horn, and she hears the song in her soul. She recognizes the melody and reaches for her higher purpose. By answering the call of her heart, she rises into her true, authentic self. Her hand glows as she stretches out of her comfort zone to find real fulfillment.

{20}

Judgement

Journal or Meditate: What is my purpose? Which area of my life brings me the most fulfillment? How can I expand this area?

Keywords: Rebirth, transformation, awakening, redemption, opportunity

Manifesting Tip: Is your heart yearning to achieve this goal? Does it feel like your calling? This card requires reflection around the reasons you're pursuing this dream. Did someone else think it would be good for you? Dig deeper to find the burning desire that comes from your soul rather than your ego.

Zodiac/Astrology Connection: Pluto—Pluto represents the underworld and treasures buried deep in the subconscious. It's calling you to search within for dreams you may not be consciously aware of. Bring them to the surface to find fulfillment.

{21}
The World

This is the completion of the Major Arcana. It represents the fulfillment of goals and dreams and signals a completed project or cycle in your life. The World card may also be a nudge to look ahead. The Universe is ready to give you the world, but only you can decide what it will include. The World is not a finish line or an ending—it is a successful completion that leads you to begin again. Take a leap of faith.

She sits in the center, cocreating her new reality with the Universe. Building a future that is filled with light and possibility, she makes room for miracles and manifests without limits.

Journal or Meditate: What are the completions of goals and dreams in my life, and what feelings did I experience? What can I manifest next? How do I use the positive emotions as a catalyst.

{21}
The World

Keywords: Completion, attainment, enlightenment, infinity, celebration, fulfilment, satisfaction.

Manifesting Tip: Although this card could represent the completion of your dream, it also welcomes you to start envisioning the next goal. Recognize that the cycles never end. One dream opens to the next. Plan for this transition. Celebrate the conclusion of one accomplishment and welcome the new beginning on the horizon.

Zodiac/Astrology Connection: Saturn—the ringed planet is associated with achievements, productiveness, and destiny. It also represents the culmination of long-term plans.

5

The Minor Arcana

As we discussed earlier, the Minor Arcana cards reflects aspects of you and your life more so than events happening to you. Because of this, they're separated into the four elements representing the four aspects of your life.

You might also notice that since these cards are more personal to you, the symbolism when you turn the Minor Arcana cards becomes more important than the traditional meanings. For this reason, you'll find the card symbols mentioned first.

As we journey through the traditional meanings of the cards, you'll also find journaling prompts to help you discover your own personal connection to each card. You can also see the cards in color at the back of the book.

CUPS

The suit of Cups symbolizes the element of Water and represents the cycle of emotions. Imagine the way water is always moving downstream or how the ocean's tide is always changing—our emotions flow in a similar fluid fashion. The Cup cards reflect this fluidity as we move through all the facets of love. The element of Water represents all kinds of love: romantic, familial, and platonic.

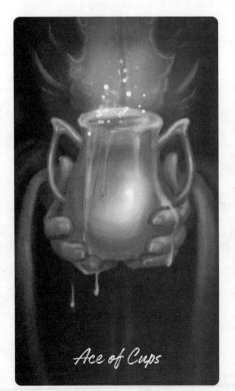

Ace of Cups

Ace of Cups

The Ace is the beginning of a new cycle of love. Her cup is overflowing with gratitude, and the green robe represents her heart chakra. The water bubbles with possibility. This is the start of something wonderful. New relationships and new passions are brewing.

This could be a new, loving partner or a passion project. If you're already in a romantic relationship, this card may also inspire a rekindling of passion. It's important to be heart focused as you say yes to new opportunities. Be willing to step out of old, stagnant waters and into the rush of a new stream of emotion.

Journal or Meditate: It's time for things that I love. What new passion do I want to welcome into my world?

Keywords: Joy, love, positivity, beauty, pleasure, fertility

Manifesting Tip: Lead with your heart as you plan your next goal. What will bring you the most love and joy? Consider manifesting new friendships or maybe dating. If you're already in a relationship, start a new cycle of love, such as planning an anniversary getaway. It's time to give your heart something to look forward to.

Two of Cups

Two of Cups

Their hands are bound with a glowing infinity sign. This is a healthy, equal, loving partnership. The golden flower tattoos are jasmine, representing eternal and unconditional love, the lush green background symbolizes the heart chakra, and the infinity symbol binds them together in a soulmate union.

The Two of Cups represents a joyful connection between two people and a very healthy partnership. This card could indicate a new relationship coming into your life or validate the one you're currently in.

If you are already in a relationship, this can be a reminder to express your love openly. Remind them how much they mean to you.

Journal or Meditate: What do I want in loving relationship? What can I do to deepen my relationship and show my partner how much I value them?

Keywords: Relationships, bond, partnership, balance, equality, joy

Manifesting Tip: Time to manifest some romance or partnerships into your life. If you're in a relationship, make time to talk and deepen your communication. Reaffirm the depth of your emotions. If you're open to love, plan outings to places and events where you could meet someone with similar interests. You may be receiving a nudge to find a partner to help you with your current goals, someone you can trust. Your heart knows. Listen.

Three of Cups

Three of Cups

Three friends dance together, laughing as they raise their cups in celebration of their friendship. Romance may come and go, but true friendship lasts a lifetime. The rainbows hop between them signifying joy, hope, and happiness.

This card is a reminder to reconnect with the people who know you best and appreciate the special enduring love of true friendship. If you're looking to make new friends, now is the time. Be open and participate in activities you enjoy. Surround yourself with like-minded souls and strive to make connections that empower you, and who you, in turn, can support too.

Journal or Meditate: How can I be a better friend to others?

Keywords: Friendship, joy, happiness, confidence, vulnerability

Manifesting Tip: It might be time to widen your friend circle. Look for events online or plan one of your own. How can you reach new like-minded people? Brainstorm ideas. This could also be a nudge to reach out to current friends and see if you can help support their dreams. There is magic and power when friends band together for a common goal.

Four of Cups

Four of Cups

The green of her dress represents the envy and jealousy in her heart. She's so busy concentrating on what the others have that she's neglecting her full cup of blessings right beside her. Divine inspiration bubbles, awaiting her to take a drink.

Remember that comparison is the thief of joy. This card is a reminder from Spirit to shift your focus from other people's gifts and accomplishments and devote your attention to your own path. Count your blessings to magnify your gratitude, then move forward on your unique journey to reclaim inner peace and harmony within.

Journal or Meditate: What are five things I love in my life, and how can I magnify my gratitude for each one?

Keywords: Contemplation, introspection, expectations, jealousy, comparison, envy

Manifesting Tip: Be sure your goal is centered on you. Life isn't a competition. It doesn't matter if your dream takes longer to manifest than it did for someone else. Your path is uniquely yours, unfolding for your highest good. You are in the right place at the right time. If pursuing your dream isn't bringing you joy, re-examine your reasons for chasing it. Make certain they're in alignment with your heart and not just what others have been doing.

Five of Cups

With her head in her hands, she weeps over her spilled cups. The blue drapes represent her deep emotions, and her red dress is the passion and drama of grief. But all is not lost. Two cups remain if she chooses to see them beside her.

This is the card of grief and loss, but the Universe is offering comfort in the memories that fill the remaining cups. When you find yourself grieving a loss, whether it be a person, pet, job, or relationship, comfort is found in acknowledging what you still have. Cherish the memories. Count these precious blessings to find solace and heal.

Journal or Meditate: How can I best support myself while my heart heals?

Keywords: Despair, loss, sadness, grief, desolation

Manifesting Tip: You may have hit an obstacle and feel like you've lost your dream forever, but this is a temporary setback. Shift your focus to the blessings you've already manifested along the way. Turn your attention to what's working instead of beating yourself up over a perceived mistake. Learn from the situation and give yourself some grace as you move forward again.

Five of Cups

Six of Cups

She sits in a meadow with her inner child. They're surrounded by poppies and lupine flowers, which represent happy memories as they reflect on the past. The flowers are in bloom, and the dreamy clouds glide across a bright blue sky, symbolizing the emotions connected with her past.

This card is full of nostalgia, but if you look closely, the scene is almost *too* perfect. Every flower is in full bloom; this perfect synchronicity rarely happens in nature. Our memories are usually not completely realistic. If you catch yourself living in the past, keep in mind that you may be omitting the struggles you endured from your memory. Because the Six of Cups is the element of Water, it's often about past relationships. Use this time to process and forgive, but don't live in yesterday.

Journal or Meditate: How can my memories of my past impact my present? What have I learned?

Keywords: Nostalgia, childhood, memories, reflection

Manifesting Tip: You might be spending too much time looking back at previous accomplishments instead of daring to dream of something new. Fear and doubt may whisper that you can't repeat such amazing, good feelings, but the Universe has even

Six of Cups

bigger things in store. Gratitude for your past blessings is a positive thing, but now is the time to allow hope to lead you back into the present, so you can focus on the future.

Seven of Cups

She is presented with so many miraculous opportunities to manifest into her life, and she only needs to choose one. Material wealth, personal growth, emotional well-being, health, and knowledge can all be hers once she decides which path will bring her the most joy.

The time to manifest is now, but because you have free will, the choice of what you'd like to bring into your life is yours alone. Cups symbolize the element of water and represent your emotions, so focus on the dream that will bring you the most joy and love. Lead with your heart in this choice.

Journal or Meditate: What would I like to manifest and bring into my life, and one which brings me the most joy? Trust your intuition. You'll make the right choice.

Keywords: Imagination, fantasy, possibility, creativity, visualization, dream

Manifesting Tip: Drop everything and dream. Even if your current goals haven't come to fruition

Seven of Cups

yet, visualize what your life will look like once they're a reality. Brainstorm what you want to manifest next. What will bring you the most joy and love? Lead with your heart. It doesn't need to be rational. Anything is possible. Daydreaming is not a waste of time.

Eight of Cups

She's poised to begin a new journey of love. The cups stand behind her, representing the lessons and love she carries with her into the future. The ship on the horizon is a new adventure. Get ready to set sail again.

Leave the emotional baggage behind and step into a new future. Perhaps you lost a partner though death or divorce, or maybe it was a career that you adored. The Universe is nudging you to get back into the water. A new, bright future filled with love awaits. You are worthy of bliss.

Eight of Cups

Journal or Meditate: What's holding me back from opening my heart again? What lessons have I learned that will help me in my new future?

Keywords: Spiritual journey, new beginnings, loss, forward movement, encouragement

Manifesting Tip: Your dream has brought you to this new opportunity. You may not have seen this journey coming. Say yes. Not only will you grow but you will love every second of the adventure. Everything you have learned and loved in your past will support you in this new endeavor. Be a bold explorer and follow your heart.

Nine of Cups

She's racing toward her dream. Will it be all she hopes for, or will it be unfulfilling? She won't know until she gets there. Her wish is made, and now is the time to see if it's granted.

The Nine of Cups is right at the edge of a completed cycle of love. Depending on your intention when you pulled the card, this may indicate that your biggest wishes are on the cusp of coming true or that your situation won't quite reach the pinnacle you had hoped for. Trust your intuition as you journey down the path to your fulfillment.

Journal or Meditate: What did I wish for? How is it manifesting in my life? Am I still on target?

Nine of Cups

Keywords: Material success, achievement, contentedness, fulfillment, recenter, assessment

Manifesting Tip: You are so close to manifesting your new reality. Visualize it as if it's already here. Engage your heart chakra to boost your vibration. Stay passionate and don't give up. Even if you've been disappointed in the past, do not allow doubt into your consciousness. Remain focused on your dream and face each day with eager anticipation of its fulfillment.

Ten of Cups

The happily ever after is here. She has manifested a family, a home, and a blissful life filled with love that is built upon equality and respect. The cat beside her symbolizes healthy boundaries, and the rainbow overhead represents happiness, hope, and good fortune.

You made it. Contentment and a loving partnership or a completed project that makes your heart sing are yours. With this enlightenment also comes the call to continue your growth. Life is made up of cycles. The completion of a cycle is also an invitation to begin another.

Ten of Cups

Journal or Meditate: What have I learned about love and friendship? How can I carry this gratitude into my next dream?

Keywords: Happiness, family, joy, beauty, love, peace, achievement, completion

Manifesting Tip: Your cup is overflowing with gratitude as your dream unfolds before your eyes.

Drink it in and recognize you are worthy of this bliss. Cherish this moment and hold on to the memory as you begin your next manifestation cycle. With each dream that becomes a reality, your confidence will grow and your grateful heart will attract even more blessings.

Page of Cups

Her laughter is contagious as a goldfish leaps from her cup. She smiles and joyfully accepts all the magic around her. She is a dreamer and allows her heart to lead the way. The fish represents her happiness as well as good fortune.

This card is calling you to honor your inner child. What did you love when you were small, and how can you work some of that joy into your daily life now? When you giggle and make time for playful activities, it raises your vibration and attracts more magic and serendipity into your life.

Journal or Meditate: What was my big love when I was a child? How can I honor my inner child today and play today?

Keywords: Artistry, creativity, inspiration, passion, youth

Page of Cups

Manifesting Tip: Have more fun. You might be working too hard to meet your goals, affecting your positive vibration. To rectify this imbalance, honor your inner child. Add a healthy dose of something playful from your childhood into the mix and watch the joy radiating from your heart begin to *attract* your dreams instead of you *chasing* them. Playfulness is a good idea right now.

Knight of Cups

With his cup raised high, this knight is eager to claim his love, but if you look closely, his horse has no bridle. There are no reins for him to guide his own path. His horse is blanketed in blue to represent emotions, and the hills are bright green, symbolizing the heart chakra.

Knight of Cups

Knights in tarot are impulsive and impetuous, which is not always a bad thing; however, this card is a nudge from Spirit to slow down. You may be a romantic with your heart on your sleeve, but don't settle for the first person who crosses your path. If you're already in a relationship, this card could also be a reminder to offer a romantic gesture and let your partner know they are loved and appreciated.

Journal or Meditate: What does a loving relationship look like to me? Have I rushed into relationships too quickly in the past? Which lessons can I carry into the future? Try writing a list of what you want from a relationship and manifest it instead of chasing it.

Keywords: Connection, charm, romance, dreams, sociability, infatuation

Manifesting Tip: Your emotions are running high, but are they taking you closer to your dream? This card could be warning you to not let your emotions get the best of you as you face an obstacle in your path, or it could be encouraging you to give your heart free rein to race forward and claim your dreams. Trust your intuition based on your intention when you pulled this card.

Queen of Cups

Queen of Cups

Her throne sits within the lush green of her heart chakra. She is a lover of the arts and in tune with her emotions but at times can be so enraptured with them that she loses herself. Staring into the cup, she is disconnected from the present and misses the admirer passing by behind her.

The Queen of Cups represents feminine, nurturing energy. Everyone carries this ability. You are very in touch with your heart, a strong intuition, creativity, and the ability to often sense how others are feeling. Sometimes those gifts can be overpowering and leave you withdrawn. Remember that love is not an object to be obtained—you must participate and cultivate your relationships. Love is meant to be shared and nurtured, not possessed.

Journal or Meditate: How can I actively show my love and appreciation for those I care for? How can I be more present?

Keywords: Intuition, emotional awareness, confidence, introspective, distance

Manifesting Tip: Your intuition is calling, but are you listening? Trust your gut as you navigate the opportunities crossing your path. Whatever decisions you make, put your heart into the choice. Emotions can be messy, but right now you need to tap into that passion even if it means you need to enforce boundaries. Don't sacrifice your needs to avoid conflict.

King of Cups

King of Cups

The King of Cups has a big heart and sincerely cares for others. This can be his greatest strength when he is bold enough to be open. He sits on his throne surrounded by water, yet refuses to get in. A ship of opportunity is passing him by, but he is unwilling to take another chance. It's time for him to open his heart again and remember why love is worth the risk.

The King of Cups represents masculine energy that we all can channel. While you're deeply emotional and kind, you can also be prone to moodiness. Once your heart is broken, you might struggle to offer it again. Love means understanding others, and at times, offering forgiveness. Address problems with a kind heart. Don't ignore them until it breaks.

Journal or Meditate: How can I be more forgiving and lead with my heart?

Keywords: Kindness, responsibility, calm, love, forgiveness, second chances

Manifesting Tip: Get creative. Are your emotions feeling raw lately? Manifesting is a marathon, not a sprint, and even those with the most positive outlooks can sometimes feel frustrated or defeated. Others look to you for encouragement, and you may feel like your well of inspiration is running dry. Fill your soul with creativity and art. Listen to music or write a poem. Allow your emotions to flow, and you'll find your stride again.

PENTACLES

The suit of Pentacles symbolizes the element of Earth and represents the cycle of the material world, of health and finances. Anything you can physically touch is part of the material world we live and move in. The Pentacle cards reflect this as we move through all the facets of physical health, earthly goods, career, and financial earnings.

Ace of Pentacles

The seeds of a divinely authorized cycle of material growth are freshly planted. From seed, to sprout, to bloom, the roots are spreading, grounded into the earth for strength. The petals are opening to a new day. Yellow and orange glow from the pentacle bulb, signifying passion and joy for this new journey, and the daffodil flower represents a new beginning.

Ace of Pentacles

This could be the time for a new income stream or a new health regimen. Abundance in all material forms is beginning to blossom. You've planted the seeds; now is the time to tend them. Your dreams are growing before your eyes.

Journal or Meditate: What new dreams do I want to harvest and bring into my life?

Keywords: Positivity, abundance, possibilities, career, financial gain, beginnings

Manifesting Tip: Now is the perfect time to begin. Abundance is all around you. If you are manifesting a new income stream or better health, start researching. You have all the tools and knowledge you need to walk this new path. Trust that the Universe is ready to deliver your dreams. Keep sending energy in that direction by taking steps toward a new business venture or new, healthier lifestyle.

Two of Pentacles

She holds two glowing pentacles, both full of potential, but it's tough to keep them balanced. The green mossy rocks behind her represent manifesting potential if she can focus and stabilize her energy.

You may be trying to juggle too many tasks at once, making it tough to keep your life balanced. Just because you *can* multitask doesn't mean you do your best work that way. You might need to make a choice when it comes to income streams or your health. Decide where to put your energy so you're not spread so thin. Maintain your focus to be sure nothing is dropped.

Two of Pentacles

Journal or Meditate: How can I better balance my priorities right now? What is my intuition guiding me to choose?

Keywords: Balance, harmony, rhythms, patterns, priorities

Manifesting Tip: You've got a lot on your plate and may need to focus on a single path or risk spreading yourself too thin. Remember that what's meant for you will not pass you by. Stay grounded in your decision-making without allowing doubts or scarcity mindset to make decisions for you. Making a choice doesn't mean you can never circle back to the other options. You're just prioritizing the goals on the way to your dream.

Three of Pentacles

The three women work together to plant the seeds and seedlings for a new future. The central woman's green dress signifies manifestation, and the yellow sunlight shining through the window behind them represents their delight in cocreating. They each bring their own unique talents and knowledge to the table.

Now is the time to network with your friends. Embrace teamwork and collaboration. If you're looking for a new job, reach out to your friends to see if they know of an opening. If you're considering a new exercise or diet plan, partner up with friends for mutual support.

Journal or Meditate: Where can I encourage collaboration in my life to grow a more abundant future?

Three of Pentacles

Keywords: Craftsmanship, collaborative, teamwork, dedication, networking

Manifesting Tip: Your friends can add to your efforts. Networking with others will also reveal new opportunities for abundance that you may not have realized existed. By getting friends involved in your project, you'll also be expanding your reach. Allow for this expansion. Now is the time to team up for success.

Four of Pentacles

Although there is an abundant harvest all around her, she clings to her purse, unwilling to purchase or enjoy it. She's missing the beauty and bounty the earth has offered because she has placed too much importance on money and material things.

You may be struggling with a scarcity mindset, but being a miser does not bring safety or security. Don't be so afraid of loss that you miss the wonders and opportunities around you. Money is energy. Send it out and welcome it back to you again. Remember that you control your money, not the other way around. If this card is drawn relating to well-being, you might consider volunteering to help others and raise your vibration.

Four of Pentacles

Journal or Meditate: Which areas of my life can I invest in?

Keywords: Scarcity, gift giving, safety, uptightness, fear

Manifesting Tip: Stop holding on so tightly. Scarcity and fear shrink our world, encouraging us to think smaller. Resist this tendency. Journal about the times the Universe surprised you with abundance to help banish the doubts. The more you trust and continue to grow, the sooner your dream will become your reality.

Five of Pentacles

Five of Pentacles

She sits in the snow while the warmth of the tree house is only steps away. The key is right there if she would only turn around and take it. The opportunity for financial security and better health is nearby.

There are opportunities waiting for you behind that door. Do not choose to remain out in the cold. Take the key or knock, and it will be opened to you. Fear or feelings of being left out may make you hesitant to take the initiative, but this card encourages you not to remain an outsider looking in. Open the door to new opportunities. Don't allow fear to hold you back.

Journal or Meditate: How can I empower myself to ask for what I need?

Keywords: Vulnerability, fear, pursuit, self-advocacy, loner

Manifesting Tip: Don't be afraid to knock on some doors. You may feel discouraged that your progress has slowed, but you don't have to feel like an outsider. If you're willing to ask for help, it will be granted. Rejection is only a certainty if you never make the request. Seek out those who can impact your journey. You don't have to wander alone in the cold.

Six of Pentacles

Six of Pentacles

She offers her bounty to another in need with a smile and open heart. Her dress is pink, symbolizing compassion and love. Her necklace is made of gold pentacles, representing abundance and good health.

Now is the time to give back. Donate your time or money to others. Giving reflects your gratitude to the Universe for the many blessings in your life. It's also a way to build your trust in the universal law of attraction. When you give, you also receive. Compassion and a generous spirit will kindle even more prosperity in your world. This card can also signal that if you have needs, they will be met.

Journal or Meditate: How can I get involved and show my gratitude through giving of my time or money?

Keywords: Charity, generosity, giving and receiving support, balance

Manifesting Tip: Pay it forward. Offer time or treasure to help others. This not only spreads light through the world but it also sends a wave of abundant energy to the Universe for the Law of Attraction to match. Even if you don't have much extra money, by giving your time or even a small amount to others in need, you're sending out positive energy that reinforces your own abundance.

Seven of Pentacles

Seven of Pentacles

She's tended her fields, and the crop will be bountiful. The bird in the tree represents her spirit guides and angels always nearby. She watches for signs, knowing the Universe will alert her when the time is right to reap the abundance she has planted.

This card is a reminder that the bountiful harvest you've planted in your life is about to reach its full potential. Divine timing is at work, and your dream is at hand. You're almost there! This is a good time to rest and reflect on how far you've come.

Journal or Meditate: Where was I when I began this cycle of growth? Where am I now? What outcome am I manifesting?

Keywords: Harvest, decision, contemplation, reflection, potential

Manifesting Tip: Reflect on your progress. When you take notice of how far you have come on your manifesting journey, you can then plot out the next chapter in your life's story. By looking over your accomplishments, you recognize the growth and prepare for even bigger things. All the seeds you've planted are beginning to ripen and bear fruit.

Eight of Pentacles

Eight of Pentacles

She stands with her prize-winning harvest. Although she's not the champion yet, her growth and progress are being recognized. Mastership is right around the corner, and with determination, she continues to pursue her dreams. The oversized vegetables are a reminder that anything is possible. The only limits are the ones you impose on yourself.

You are becoming a master of your craft. Study, practice, learn from mentors and teachers, and continue to grow. If it's worth having, then it's worth the effort to achieve it. Steady progress will lead to a prosperous future.

Journal or Meditate: How can I expand my abilities to improve my craft and skills?

Keywords: Apprenticeship, dedication, skill, artistry, mastery

Manifesting Tip: You have worked hard to learn and grow, and now you can see the fruits of your labors taking shape. Seize that confidence and dream even bigger. Expand your vision. You are capable and deserving of every blessing coming your way. Embrace the opportunity to use your new skills in unexpected ways.

Nine of Pentacles

She enjoys a picnic, secure in her own company. The sunflowers represent her joy, and the pentacles on her dress symbolize the welcome financial and physical security she has manifested in her life. As she lifts the beautiful grapes, she whispers her gratitude and breathes in the sweet smell of success.

This cycle of abundance is nearing completion. Take a breath and enjoy the progress you've made. Not only is this a prosperous time but you have built it honorably. This is a time to enjoy the journey. The final accomplishment of your goals will be here soon enough.

Journal or Meditate: Time to reflect on my progress and recommit to the final push toward my dream. How can I stay inspired and continue walking in a path of gratitude?

Keywords: Enjoyment, solitude, accomplishment, self-sufficiency, discipline, appreciation

Manifesting Tip: You've worked hard to reach this point. Breathe. You've laid the foundation. Now allow your destiny to unfold before your eyes. Continue your forward progress while also recognizing how far you've come. Your dream is nearly fulfilled. Keep the faith.

Ten of Pentacles

It's raining pentacles as she dances in the flood of prosperity. Her work has paid off, and it's time to celebrate. She is present and positive, knowing that her needs will be more than met—they will be surpassed. The bright-green background symbolizes successful manifesting.

Financial abundance, physical health, and material success are assured. Your efforts have manifested in good fortune and improved well-being as you complete the pentacles cycle. Celebrate and allow gratitude to fill your heart as you prepare to go after your next big dream.

Ten of Pentacles

Journal or Meditate: Celebrate how far you have come during this cycle of growth. Focus on gratitude and delight to raise your vibration.

Keywords: Success, achievement, fulfillment, peace

Manifesting Tip: Celebrate the abundant new reality that you have cocreated with the Universe. Your energy and efforts have manifested a bright future filled with material abundance, joy, and opportunity. Take this mastery into your next cycle. Invest in your future goals and dreams, knowing you are a conscious cocreator who attracts good fortune.

Page of Pentacles

Page of Pentacles

He's in a cave, surrounded by the abundance of the earth. As he ponders the glowing crystal overhead, his potential is limitless. Anything is possible. His green shirt symbolizes both his heart chakra and the color of manifesting. Which career will blossom from his big dreams?

The page represents your inner child with the curiosity and eagerness of youth. What did you think your career would be when you were younger? How can you add some of that enthusiasm into your current work endeavors? Watch for that spark of inspiration when it comes to your health and money. When you honor your inner child, you raise your vibration and attract more joy.

Journal or Meditate: When I was younger, how did I imagine I would earn my money versus my career today? How can I bring in some of that youthful energy into my daily work?

Keywords: Youth, ambition, progress, adventure, resourcefulness, detail, focus

Manifesting Tip: You have laid your plans, but did you include fun and play? Enjoy every day and each step of the path you're traveling. Do not put happiness on hold until the dream is accomplished. Life is the journey, not the destination. Tap into your inner child's energy and make this work into a game in order to keep your vibration up even when obstacles get in your way.

Knight of Pentacles

The knight is so eager for the crystals that he leaps into the cavern, leaving his rope tied to the saddle behind him. He dives in with both feet and no exit plan. The purple crystals validate that this is a divinely inspired opportunity. Slow down to consider everything before you jump in.

Knight of Pentacles

Knights rush in where others fear to tread. They're full of impulsive energy, eager to take action, but often lack the follow-through to finish. This card could be telling you that while your plans for a new income stream or fitness aspirations are potentially valuable, it is best to slow down and plot your course for your ultimate success.

Journal or Meditate: How can I channel my enthusiasm into a viable plan of action? Have I been thinking about improving my health and finances? What steps can I take to make my aspirations a reality?

Keywords: Integrity, work ethic, responsibility, impulsiveness, distraction

Manifesting Tip: Perseverance is called for right now. Stay dedicated to your plan and focus on completing each step along the way. Your efforts will be rewarded as you focus on the goal without being distracted or pulled off course by other intentions. You have the stamina to see this through.

Queen of Pentacles

Her green dress represents her abundant spirit and ability to manifest health and money. Even the toadstools glow in her presence. However, her face and disheveled hair reveal she might be overworked and spreading herself too thin.

The queen may validate your abundance and charitable heart for family and friends. This is a feminine nurturing energy of healing that everyone can possess. You care deeply for the financial and physical well-being of others, but sometimes this can be draining. Be sure to maintain healthy boundaries so that you don't sacrifice more than you should. Asking for help when you need it is important.

Journal or Meditate: Are you nurturing yourself as much as you care for others? How can you show yourself that same healing compassion?

Keywords: Success, abundance, fulfilment, self-care, boundaries

Manifesting Tip: You are practical and make the most of the resources at your disposal. The seeds of abundance you have planted are beginning to grow. Remember that you don't have to face this journey alone. Enlist the help of others to tend this garden of possibility so that you don't get burned out. Be resourceful with your time and energy.

Queen of Pentacles

King of Pentacles

The King of Pentacles has manifested his fortune and shares his prosperity with those he loves. No one leaves his table with an empty belly. The green background reflects his ability to attract material riches and his brown suit reflects the grounded element of earth.

This is a card of abundance and confidence. A good omen for business dealings and contracts. This is masculine energy of authority and judgment. Keep in mind that all problems cannot be solved with money alone. Too much focus on material wealth can rob you of emotional connections.

Journal or Meditate: How can I better embrace my connection to prosperity? Am I seeking out opportunities to help others?

Keywords: Success, industriousness, generosity, reliability, power

Manifesting Tip: You have mastered manifesting all that you desire through your ability to remain grounded and focused on the tasks that must be accomplished. This ability gives you the assurance that you can cocreate whatever you deem necessary. Now use your gifts and treasures to help others. Your reliability and commitment to a goal make you a brilliant leader for others.

King of Pentacles

WANDS

The suit of Wands symbolizes the element of Fire and represents the cycle of action. Passion and desire burn through this cycle as you take on projects and make things happen. The Wand cards represent that spark of inspiration that smolders into a bonfire of activity until a project is completed.

Ace of Wands

A new cycle of action and inspiration has begun. The fire of creation and an explosion of creativity is upon you. This is a divinely authorized beginning of a new cycle of activity. The flames beckon you to come closer and take the wand. The time is now.

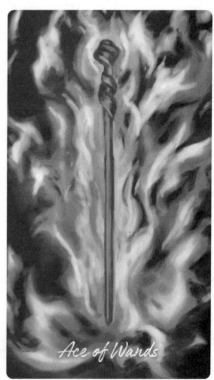

Fire is the embodiment of passion. Channel that frenetic energy into your new project or career. You have been contemplating this endeavor and the timing for a while now. This card is your validation to move forward. Harness your enthusiasm and begin without any further hesitation.

Journal or Mediation: What steps can I take today to begin my new project?

Keywords: Passion, creation, beginnings

Manifesting Tip: Take action. The spark of inspiration has the potential to transform your reality. Unlimited potential is yours, so dream big. Each step in the direction of your dream provides a wave of prosperous energy. This is not a time for hesitation. The first step is always the hardest, but it must be taken. The time is now.

Two of Wands

It's time to make a choice. She could play a masterpiece or paint one. The globe beside her represents a world of opportunity, and the candles glow with eager anticipation, ready to light the fire of creation. Once she decides where she will focus her energies, the adventure will begin.

The world can be yours, but you must choose your next course of action or risk spreading yourself too thin. This is not a time to split your focus. Trust your instincts and take action on the goal that means the most to you right now. Follow your passion.

Journal or Meditate: Think about your potential projects and action plans. Which one lights the fire in your soul?

Two of Wands

Keywords: Preparation, choices, desire, dreams, aspiration, ambition, decision

Manifesting Tip: Progress has begun, and now is the time to plot your course ahead. Make plans to reach your dream, but remember to allow for Spirit to provide what you need. You are in partnership with the energy of the Divine. Allow it to inspire your actions as you plan your future. Anything is possible. Envision your success, and it will come to fruition.

Three of Wands

The choice has been made, and his journey has begun. He is ready to climb the stairs and step through the door on the way to his next dream. The fire of passion pushes through the emotions and fears as he moves out of his comfort zone and on to his next adventure.

Enough plotting and planning—this card marks the beginning of your new action cycle. You've mapped your course, and now it's time to implement it. The future is in sight, and your efforts will pay off. It all starts with that first step.

Journal or Meditate: What has been holding me back? How can I take a step closer to my dream today?

Three of Wands

Keywords: Strategy, discovery, implementation, action

Manifesting Tip: There are so many opportunities ahead. Don't get lost in indecision. Stay focused on your plan and continue to take action. Hesitation and delays could snuff out the passion for your dream. Each completed task brings you closer to your ultimate success. Avoid being distracted by too many options. Wise choices will lead to positive action steps.

Four of Wands

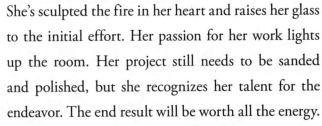

She's sculpted the fire in her heart and raises her glass to the initial effort. Her passion for her work lights up the room. Her project still needs to be sanded and polished, but she recognizes her talent for the endeavor. The end result will be worth all the energy.

This card marks your first taste of internal validation for your new action cycle. This is the moment you realize you will excel and all your efforts or newly learned skills were worth the time and energy. This is a celebration that you are on the right path.

Journal or Meditate: How can I honor my progress so far on my new project? Where can I continue to grow on the next part of my journey?

Four of Wands

Keywords: Celebration, validation, inspiration, harmony, refinery, continuation

Manifesting Tip: You're making measurable progress on your big goal. Take time to give yourself some recognition. Celebrating also raises your vibration to attract even more successes. Make a gratitude list of all the blessings you've had so far as encouragement to continue this road with eager anticipation of what's in store for the future.

Five of Wands

The volcano is erupting, but instead of working together to control the lava flow, they're fighting among themselves, each believing their plan of action is the best. Passion is bubbling, but the lack of unified direction may jeopardize everything.

This card is halfway through the activity cycle of wands and represents the chaos that erupts when conflict and ambitions clash. If you are working with a team on a project, this may be the time to remind everyone of the original mission and brainstorm a unified path forward. If you're working on a project alone, this card can be a nudge from the Universe to focus your efforts and regroup. Stop trying to do everything all at once.

Five of Wands

Journal or Meditate: Which path will lead to my goal? Time to refocus and recommit to the outcome I desire.

Keywords: Competition, conflict, obstacles, tension, refocus

Manifesting Tip: Obstacles are opportunities for growth. There may be some chaos on your path, but you are capable of unifying the efforts of those involved. Refocus on your original dream. You may have lost your way. Use this opportunity to think outside the box to find new solutions you might not have considered before. This isn't a failure; it's a course correction.

Six of Wands

Six of Wands

Her town throws a parade in celebration of her triumphant return. Confetti and flags herald her victory. Even the bright-blue sky signals her potential. She smiles, knowing she is worthy of their praise and recognition.

Success is yours. The Six of Wands represents outward recognition of your progress toward your goal. You are winning hard-fought battles on the way to the completion of this cycle, and others are taking notice. Expect awards, raises, testimonials, and referrals as those around you recognize your progress and growth. You are worthy and deserving of the accolades.

Journal or Meditate: How can I best continue to learn and expand my skills as I continue to grow? What's my next challenge?

Keywords: Success, victory, reward, accomplishment, expansion, recognition

Manifesting Tip: Step into the spotlight and accept the accolades of others. Enjoy this sweet victory on the journey to your big dream. Renew your faith in your path and your abilities. Cherish this moment of validation to light your way if you find yourself struggling in the future. You are transforming your circumstances for the highest good for all.

Seven of Wands

She stands on her own as a determined, battle-tested warrior. Although she may be exhausted, she fights on bravely and is unstoppable. Her passion for her mission glows brightly like the fire smoldering around her.

It's time to face the challenges brewing around you. You may feel abandoned or isolated, but you don't need to carry this burden alone. Ask for help if you need it, but do not give up. This is merely a bump in the road on your path to success. This is not a time to be complacent. Keep up the fight.

Seven of Wands

Journal or Meditate: What is standing in my way right now? How can I move past it, and who can help me?

Keywords: Defensiveness, bravery, protection, competitor, strength, fighter, assistance

Manifesting Tip: Are you feeling exhausted and burnt out? Do not give up. Dig deep and persevere through adversity. You might consider asking a trusted friend for help right now. Having someone to help you past this spot is wise. Be present as you battle through this rough patch and watch for solutions to present themselves.

Eight of Wands

Eight of Wands

She sits on the stairs, staring into the flames. Her goal is within reach, but she hesitates to move, struggling between a lack of focus and procrastination.

You may be exhausted or overwhelmed, but it is important to push forward and finish your project. The temptation to put things off is growing, but this card is your nudge from the Universe to jump up and take action. No more stalling. Take a breath and get back on the road to your ultimate goal. Push through your doubts and fears. You know what you need to do. Now is the time.

Journal or Meditate: Why am I hesitating? Procrastination is often the mask that fear wears. I can overcome anything once I face it head-on.

Keywords: Change, action, velocity, determination, exhaustion, perseverance

Manifesting Tip: You may need to find your momentum again. It's time for a pep talk. Do not allow procrastination and excuses to keep you from progressing. Your dream is in sight. Try journaling out your concerns so that you can see them for what they are— fear. Release the doubt and reignite your passion for this journey. Transformation is on the horizon.

Nine of Wands

She may be physically and mentally exhausted, but her goal is in sight. Nothing can stop her now as she climbs the mountain guided by her intuition and in the flow of the Universe. The crystals glow green, matching her shirt, as she manifests her future, cocreating with Spirit. She has the strength and determination to finish her quest.

Don't give up now! The finish line is in sight, and your dream will be manifested as long as you

Nine of Wands

keep moving forward. One step at a time. Keep persevering. You've got this.

Journal or Meditate: I dip back into the passion I had at the beginning of this journey. I remember why I started this project and what new adventures are waiting at the finish line. I take the spark of excitement and use it to reach my goal.

Keywords: Courage, determination, strength, standing your ground, final push

Manifesting Tip: When you can't imagine taking another step, the Universe coaches you to push through this exhaustion. You'll be so glad you did. Your goal is at hand. Find your determination and see this project through to completion. You have come so far. Allow the insights of this journey to guide you forward until you bring your dream to fruition.

Ten of Wands

She's planted and harvested this bountiful crop but now finds herself carrying the entire bounty on her own. It's exhausting. The purple tips on each wand represent her connection to the Universe. This project is worth the effort, but the burden doesn't need to be hers alone. Spirit is ready to cocreate with her.

You're so close to the finish line, but you might be taking on too much at once. Cocreation with the Universe means that you also need to surrender and allow Spirit to take the lead. Asking for help is not a weakness. Lighten your load, or you'll miss the beauty all around you.

Journal or Meditate: What extra baggage am I carrying around with me? What can be released so that I can finish my project?

Keywords: Overburdened, support, cocreation, release

Manifesting Tip: The weight of this goal burdens you. Perhaps you have spread yourself too thin. While you may have achieved the dream, is it sustainable? Asking for the help you need is not a weakness. What good is achieving a dream if you can't enjoy it? Hire an assistant or talk to friends to get the help you need. Lighten your workload.

Ten of Wands

Page of Wands

She is painting a wand that symbolizes the creative spark within. The colors reflect the passion and desire in her heart to create without limitations. She is unstoppable and eager to discover her talents and try new things.

The Page is a call from your inner child. They're ready to fire up your creativity and passion for projects. Tap into the energy of your younger self and think about what activities used to excite you. This is a call to honor those passions and discover ways to integrate them into your current project to reignite your delight and joy. There is power in playing. It raises your vibration and helps you to manifest more joy. Play is never wasted time.

Page of Wands

Journal or Meditate: How can I honor the passions of my youth in my current projects? Where can I dream bigger?

Keywords: New ideas, creativity, whims, impulse, play

Manifesting Tip: Dream boldly with the wonder of a child. You really can accomplish anything. Take action on that new idea. See how you can inject some fun into the process. When you please your inner child, it won't feel like work. You'll be eager to get things done, seeing each step as a closer view to your big dream.

Knight of Wands

The Knight of Wands is impetuous and ambitious but often lacks a plan to finish. He's so anxious to dive in and start his project that he forgot to tie up his horse. In the distance, the volcano smokes, but he has not even noticed and has no plans to evacuate.

You might be taking on too much at once and spreading yourself thin. Take the time to plan your projects so you can see them through to the finish line instead of losing interest and starting something new. Your passion cannot be denied, but if you are too impulsive, your many activities and projects could suffer.

Journal or Meditate: What are my passion projects, and which one should I focus on first? What steps are needed to see it through to completion?

Keywords: Boldness, recklessness, impulsivity, risk, possibility, pursuit

Manifesting Tip: You are an unstoppable force, chasing after new innovations. Beware of headstrong tendencies so that you remain true to your original path. When you focus, you can accomplish anything. Contain the impetuous energy to try everything and concentrate on the goals in front of you. If you haven't made an action plan yet, now is the time.

Knight of Wands

Queen of Wands

It is nightfall before the Queen of Wands finds time to tend her own garden. She is often so busy organizing events and doing work for others that her own projects have to wait. The blooming flowers are a testament to her multitasking abilities, but her cat is reminding her to set boundaries before she burns herself out.

Although you *can* do it all, should you? The Queen is a validation that you are always reliable for those you care about, but it's also a warning that if you don't set personal limits, your independent interests could suffer. Make space in your schedule for your passion projects too. You deserve that time.

Queen of Wands

Journal or Meditate: If I weren't being pulled in multiple directions, what would I choose to work on? How can I carve out time for that work? What boundaries do I need to set?

Keywords: Power, ability, generosity, overwhelm, boundaries, balance, self-advocacy

Manifesting Tip: How much time and energy do you put toward your own dreams? You are dedicated to helping others achieve their goals, and you excel at this. However, your dreams and passions matter too. Save some energy for your own ambitions. How can you reserve more time for your pursuits?

King of Wands

The King of Wands is a charismatic leader with a creative vision and a fiery determination to make his dreams a reality. The lion represents his courage to pursue his goals. He rises from his throne, ready to lead, inspire, and protect those he loves. His resolve to get things done can sometimes cause him not to trust others to assist. But a strong leader empowers others, and many hands make light work.

This card is a call to recognize your leadership skills and share your vision with others. Once your project is underway, allow others to support you and fight the urge to take over everything. You can accomplish more as a team.

Journal or Meditate: How can I step into leadership more? Which project needs my attention next?

Keywords: Authority, career success, leadership, delegation, inspire, confidence, step back

Manifesting Tip: This dream is bigger than you and will benefit many. As you mentor others and inspire their work, your own skills also grow. Be open to the input and suggestions of your team. Although you have the vision, other opinions could make it even brighter. It's time to empower others and consider their contributions to the whole. Welcome other viewpoints.

King of Wands

SWORDS

The suit of Swords symbolizes the element of Air and represents the cycle of thoughts and ideas. We can't see air or touch it, and yet it's vital for our survival. Your thoughts operate in the same way. They're ethereal like air, and often very real in our heads and not tangible in the real world around us. The Sword cards reflect this as we move through all the stages of our mental health and thought processes.

Ace of Swords

Ace of Swords

She clasps her sword as roses creep up the blade, symbolizing a new Spirit-led cycle of thought. Her reverent hold on the hilt represents her commitment to follow through to see that the idea becomes a reality. This new knowledge is inspiring and uplifting, guiding you down a path you hadn't considered before.

Expect a bright idea to step forward and begin a new cycle of thought. This card can also signify a moment of clarity. Your intuition is sending you aha moments to pierce the clouds of self-doubt. Seize the day.

Journal or Meditate: How can I take a step toward making my idea a reality? Am I pondering a new concept and waiting for a sign before committing to it? I can break my idea into small actionable steps and visualize the idea taking shape in my life.

Keywords: Fresh ideas, inspiration, originality, clarity, beginnings, pursuit

Manifesting Tip: A new, inspired idea is forming in your mind. As it becomes clear, watch for synchronicities and signs as the Universe guides you to take action. You will know when the timing is right if you are present and paying attention. Destiny and fate are coming together to inspire greatness.

Two of Swords

Two of Swords

She stands between two ideas, unwilling or unable to choose which one to grasp. Wearing a blindfold, she seeks to ignore the decision placed before her, remaining willfully undecided. The birds on the hilts represent her spirit guides and angels, ready to offer counsel. Above her head, the clouds are parting, allowing the enlightenment of Spirit to shine, if she chooses to see it.

It is time to stop avoiding the situation, and make a choice. Meditate on both options and trust your intuition. Be rational instead of emotional, using your head versus your heart. Avoiding this decision will not bring you closer to your goals.

Journal or Meditate: What are my ideas and the pros and cons for each one? As I meditate on the possible outcomes, I will be sure to keep my emotions at bay and use my head for this decision.

Keywords: Indecision, tension, dilemma, rationality, choice

Manifesting Tip: You may be trying to avoid making a decision. Consider the options before you and release uncertainty. Trust your intuition, and the choice will become clearer. This is a time to lead with your head and not your heart. Clarity and a peaceful state of mind will be required as you choose your path to your dreams.

Three of Swords

Three of Swords

She's heartbroken about someone or something, and the more she thinks about it, the bigger and more intense the situation becomes in her mind. The bright-red heart signifies the drama of her extreme emotions as she stares into her reflection, playing out scenarios in her head.

No one enjoys pulling the Three of Swords, but keep in mind that swords represent the element of Air. A painful situation can feel as though there is no escape. Your mind spirals until you're sure that heartbreak is imminent, no matter what you do. This drama is in your head. Often, rejection and disappointment are the Universe protecting you with a course correction. You are supported as you face every trial. This challenging time will pass.

Journal or Meditate: How many times have I looked back on a past disappointment and discovered it was actually a blessing in disguise? I will give myself time to heal and then prepare for growth.

Keywords: Grief, rumination, strife, heartbreak, betrayal, crisis

Manifesting Tip: Disappointments are not meant to stop you. Sometimes rejections and obstacles are the Universe guiding you to course-correct to something much better than you had previously envisioned. Consider this Divine protection and release your expectations to allow for something greater into your life. This struggle is only temporary.

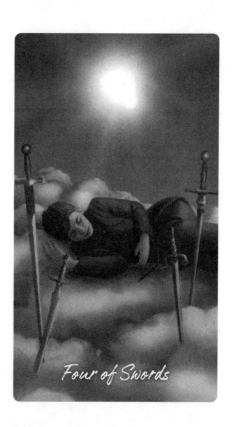

Four of Swords

He sleeps on the clouds of his dreams. His worries, concerns, and new ideas are set aside so he can rest his mind and spirit and accept the healing light of the Universe. The problems have not disappeared; they will be dealt with later. This is a time for healing.

The Four of Swords calls for a much-needed rest. Now is the time to slow down and allow your mind and body to rejuvenate. Make sure you are making enough time for sleep. If you need a nap, take one. This is self-care, not laziness.

Journal or Meditate: How can I make more time for rest? Which areas of my life can be paused to allow for extra sleep?

Keywords: Rest, meditation, relaxation, introspection, healing

Manifesting Tip: Time for meditation and rest. You need clarity, and this cannot be found when you are mentally and emotionally exhausted. Getting enough sleep is imperative while you are manifesting positive changes. Consider it self-care. Meditation will also help you to heal your spirit and prepare to welcome new cycles of growth.

Five of Swords

She carries five swords, more than she could ever wield, yet she still fears they won't be enough. The sun shines brightly, the water is calm, and there are no storms in the distance, but she is still readying for the worst.

Anxiety radiates from this card. If you find yourself waiting for the next shoe to drop, remind yourself—this is the element of Air. The battles seem epic in your head, but are they real in the world around you? Maybe it's the fear of failure whispering in your ear, but you have all the tools you need to face this moment.

Journal or Meditate: What are the fears that are weighing on me and keeping me from moving forward? Seeing them in the light of day can help me recognize them for what they are . . . air. What small steps can I take today to move past them?

Keywords: Anxiety, defense, conflation, recognition, fear, trepidation, worry

Manifesting Tip: Anxiety shrinks the world you are trying to expand. Worry is wasted energy. Combat this fear by being present and not allowing your mind to wander into the past or future. Meditate and visualize the dream life you are currently manifesting. Lose yourself in the positive emotions of the visualization until your desire for change is bigger than your fear. Then you're ready to move forward again.

Five of Swords

Six of Swords

She sits alone in a boat floating downstream but makes no effort to grab the oars and navigate. Instead, the swords at the bow of the boat represent the expectations and advice of others, and they are leading her through a river of transition to what *they* think is best for her.

Are you weighed down by the expectations of others? Accept this nudge from the Universe to grab the oars and steer your ship. This is your journey, not someone else's. Maybe you are transitioning out of a difficult situation, and it seems easier to go with the flow. However, remember that you get to *choose* to accept the advice of others. You are not *required* to do so. Take up your oars and determine your own course.

Six of Swords

Journal or Meditate: Am I feeling adrift? Have I given someone else's opinion or expectations too much influence over my future? Just because someone expects me to do something doesn't mean I don't have other options.

Keywords: Journey, pilgrimage, movement, expectation, self-assurance

Manifesting Tip: Have you been keeping your dream a secret, afraid to tell anyone for fear you might fail or disappoint them? This sends a mixed message to your subconscious as well as the

Universe. It's like expecting to fail. How can anyone support your growth if they don't know you are manifesting change? Shift your awareness and welcome change. Know you will achieve it, and then declare your intentions. Now you are steering your ship toward transformation.

Seven of Swords

She is collecting all the swords as if a battle looms ahead, yet she is alone in the chamber. Daylight filters through the window, but she does not step into the light. Is she stealing or concerned someone else might take from her first?

You may be feeling like someone is deceiving you, or perhaps you're only lying to yourself. Have you been worrying and looking over your shoulder to see if you're being exploited? Sometimes what seems real inside your mind is not a true reflection of what is happening in the world around you. It's time to change your perspective. Get out of your head to see the situation from the outside. Paranoia might be clouding your judgment.

Seven of Swords

Journal or Meditate: I need to examine my current situation from all sides, tap into my heart chakra, and trust my intuition. If my gut is telling me all is well, then trust it.

Keywords: Deception, anxiety, trust, intuition, new perspective

Manifesting Tip: You are paying too much attention to other people instead of focusing on your life's progress. What they think doesn't matter. If you are constantly worried about what someone else might say or do, eventually that worry will become your reality. Stay focused on your path. Trust that events are unfolding exactly the way they should. Have confidence in Divine timing. You are in the right place at the right time. Stop preparing for the worst.

Eight of Swords

Eight of Swords

She stands blindfolded on a mountaintop surrounded by swords. While her worries and fears leave her feeling trapped, if she removes her blindfold, the path to freedom is clear. The choice is hers to move forward.

Are you feeling stuck in an uncomfortable situation? If you believe there is no way out, this card is a nudge from the Universe to take off your blindfold and walk away. You are not a victim. As soon as you open your eyes, your path forward will be revealed. This is a call to release victimhood and step into your power. You can escape this situation anytime you choose to do so.

Journal or Meditate: What situation has me

feeling helpless or stuck? What is one step I can take today to begin my exit strategy? Change happens one choice at a time. I will take off the blindfold and free myself.

Keywords: Restrictions, limitations, unveil, new perspective

Manifesting Tip: Stop living in denial of your power. You can manifest anything. The only way to fail is to stand still, trapped behind excuses and fears. Take off the blindfold of illusion and have the courage to step into clarity. You will discover your fears were unfounded and you have the courage and strength to overcome any obstacle in your way.

Nine of Swords

Nine of Swords

She sits in her comfortable bed, exhausted but unable to settle onto her pillow and slumber. Even with her book to read, paper to write out her thoughts, and teddy bear close by, sleep still eludes her as her worries hang over her head.

This card can be a warning to get more rest, but often insomnia comes when your brain won't stop churning with distressing thoughts. If you're struggling to silence your worries, try meditating before bed, and ask your angels to carry your swords so that you can get some much-needed sleep.

Journal or Meditate: I must remember I am are never alone and always supported by the Universe and my angels and spirit guides. I write out my concerns on paper and surrender them to the Creator. With more sleep comes better mental health and coping skills.

Keywords: Troubled, overworked, release, rest, insomnia, mental exhaustion

Manifesting Tip: It's time to change your self-talk. If you find your ego whispering that you don't know enough, or you're not worthy, or other lies it might tell you, it's time to change the script. You can do this by reciting a mantra or meditate and cut the energetic cords tying you to limiting beliefs. New opportunities are on the horizon. Rest and clear your head so that you can claim your destiny.

Ten of Swords

With her head in her hands, she weeps under the burden of her worry and sorrow, but the promise of a beautiful new day is on the horizon. Although the swords impale her back, there is no blood. The bird circling overhead represents her spirit guide calling her to lift her head and see the blessing of a new beginning. This, too, shall pass.

The Ten of Swords can represent depression and painful endings, but it is also a reminder that healing is all around you. Lift your head and see the blessings beyond the disappointment. A dark night of the soul can lead to a beautiful rebirth and a new resilience. You are stronger than you know.

Journal or Meditate: I shift my focus to the blessings in my life. Keeping a gratitude journal for a few days, I write down all the bright spots in my days. Gratitude plucks the swords of disappointment from my back and replaces them with hope.

Keywords: Confusion, loss, strife, depression, hidden blessings, gratitude

Manifesting Tip: You might be feeling like your dreams will never be manifested. But don't give up. When disappointment pierces you, look for the small blessings. Miracles are all around if you look for them. Lift your eyes and, as you witness wonders around you, absorb the hope of the new day. Accept the lessons you have learned and embrace the epiphany of gratitude. You are loved and supported.

Ten of Swords

Page of Swords

The youthful page has so many ideas reflected in her sword. Where to begin? Each new thought carries the promise of a new learning adventure. This curious energy will lead her to study and accept new opportunities. The tip of the sword glows with divinely inspired thought.

Do you remember the magic of daydreaming as a child? Or the many subjects—dinosaurs, planets, animals—that piqued your interest? Now is the time to honor the curiosity of your inner child. Look for learning opportunities to tap into that youthful passion. This is a time to expand your mind and invite new adventures.

Page of Swords

Journal or Meditate: Which subjects captivated me in my youth? How long has it been since I learned something new about them? I will devote energy in that direction. I will make a list and visit a bookstore or search online for new courses to take.

Keywords: Ambition, inspiration, brightness, learning

Manifesting Tip: Explore new ideas with childlike curiosity. Be willing to learn and experience new things to enhance your manifesting journey. Who knows where a book or a new course might take you? Your dream is developing in new ways.

Be inquisitive and explore new ideas. You are an adventurer. Allow your inner child to take the lead.

Knight of Swords

The Knight of Swords is chasing his new idea with youthful eagerness and tenacity, but the sign behind him is as chaotic as his pursuit. He's forgotten his horse and races onward without directions or assistance. While the tip of his sword glows with divine inspiration, logic will only take him so far.

Knights always rush in, and the Knight of Swords is notorious for running with a new idea, but quickly loses impulsion, then interest, and finds himself with nothing to show for his efforts. Your idea has potential, but take time to plot out a plan of action. Engage both your heart and your head before you chase after this new inspiration.

Knight of Swords

Journal or Meditate: I will organize my thoughts into a coherent action plan. With each mapped-out plan, my determination and confidence in my idea will strengthen until it solidifies into a map for my bright idea to come to fruition.

Keywords: Impulsivity, confidence, fervor, follow-through, creativity, ideas

Manifesting Tip: Be adaptable when responding to situations. As you evolve in the course of your manifesting, beware not to fall into old thought patterns. Choose to respond differently. While swift reactions and responses may be natural for you, think it through and allow yourself the chance to change your behavior. Your dream is worth the effort.

Queen of Swords

Queen of Swords

With her sword in hand, the queen is a thoughtful communicator. She has clarity and brings unbiased reasoning to the table for those who seek her counsel. Her black dress represents power and wisdom and authority. This is the friend you can count on for solutions, good judgment, and wisdom.

This card is usually a validation that you are wise and eager to help others problem solve and repair miscommunications. However, it can also be a nudge from the Universe that you are living a little too much inside your head. Be sure you are outwardly communicating your thoughts and opinions when asked, instead of jumping to conclusions and judgments.

Journal or Meditate: What are situations that are affecting me or my friends and family right now? How can I help to mediate and find potential solutions?

Keywords: Intelligence, perception, wit, clarity, honesty, communication, problem-solver

Manifesting Tip: You have clarity of purpose, but manifesting also requires passion. Do not run scenarios in your head without sharing your wisdom and foresight. Your actions need to align with your ideas. Give them voice and communicate your expectations honestly with yourself and any others you might be working with.

King of Swords

As storm clouds gather, the King of Swords relies on his wisdom, represented by the owl on his arm. He is intelligent and clear-headed but at times can appear abrupt or cold because his emotions are often detached or distant. The earth tones of his suit symbolize his grounded logical thought process.

King of Swords

This card is a validation of your thoughtful wisdom and clear communication. Your standards are high, but be sure they are balanced with compassion. Be careful that your ideas do not become manipulations. Inspire others, instead of seeking to overpower.

Journal or Meditate: How can I better communicate my ideas so that my wisdom does not come across as arrogance or manipulation? How can I empower those around me?

Keywords: Grounded, rationality, communication, inspiration, wisdom

Manifesting Tip: You are a strong negotiator, and you trust your instincts. This makes you a level-headed leader and a clear communicator. Make a clear strategy to reach your goal and inspire others to get involved as well. Take time to reflect on the past and how it formed the present so that you can plan for future growth.

6

Spreads and the Communication Between the Cards

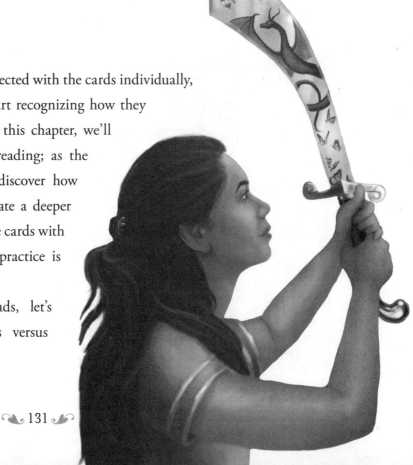

Once you have connected with the cards individually, you're ready to start recognizing how they work together. In this chapter, we'll begin with a single-card reading; as the chapter continues, you'll discover how your cards can communicate a deeper message by pulling multiple cards with different intentions. This practice is called a tarot spread.

Before discussing spreads, let's talk about upright cards versus reversals, or cards that are drawn upside down. Reversals are sometimes considered to have the opposite meaning. For example, if you drew The Sun reversed, it might mean bad luck is headed your way instead of good luck and joy. However, I trust the Universe wouldn't tell you what you *cannot* have. I believe the seventy-eight cards represent all the aspects of our lives fully on their own without the addition of reversals. That said, if reversals resonate with you, then feel free to incorporate them into the reading of your spreads. Trust your intuition.

One-Card Draw

Three of Cups

If you start with a one-card reading, try asking a question to the Universe, such as, "What do I need to know today?" or "What is my focus today?" One-card readings are a great way to gain meaningful insight as you begin your day. For example, I pulled the Three of Cups this morning with the intention of "Where should I focus my energy today?"

As my day continued, I was not surprised when I received a group text from some of my writer friends to have a virtual lunch and catch-up. After that wink from the Universe, I agreed, and we'll be video chatting next week!

Get creative with your one-card readings by asking about your career, relationship, and long-term projects you've been working on. One-card readings are an equally fantastic way to start your day with intention and end your day with reflection or, for direction, at the start of a new project or at any time of day. The options are endless.

Pulling Multiple Cards for One Question

Before getting into more complex spreads, first try drawing multiple cards and looking for ways the meanings intersect. You might try asking a question like "What do I need to know right now?" Your question prompts the story of the cards to unfold.

Here's an example of pulling five cards.

Two of Pentacles   *Page of Pentacles*   *Two of Wands*   *Ten of Pentacles*   *Justice*

Instead of searching for each individual meaning in the guide-book, try looking at the cards in front of you and listen to your intuition. Which cards draw your attention first? Did you notice first that there are two Two cards? Or did the three Pentacle cards catch your eye? Perhaps you're waiting to hear a decision about a job and are immediately drawn to the Justice card and the Ten of Pentacles. Where do you think the Two of Wands fits in? It's the only element of Fire in the spread. What do you need to take action on?

The cards tell a story based on what your intuition sees. You have to trust your intuition and allow it to translate the cards into the message you need.

Remember that there is a reason you pulled the cards. You always get the cards you need; that's why you drew them. They're doing their job when they spark an idea. As you use your deck more, your confidence will grow. You will start to see how the cards can modify the others in your spread and connect with the new meanings for you.

Your recognition of the cards and cycles is sharpened the more often you use them, so make using your cards into a daily practice.

EXERCISE

Keep a tarot journal for a week. Each day, try pulling five cards with the intention of "What do I need to know today?" Write down the cards you drew along with your initial interpretation of them. At the end of the day, reflect on how the day unfolded. At the end of the week, look over all your daily readings to build your familiarity with the cards and how they work with each other, as well as to build your confidence and trust in your intuition.

Spreads

Tarot spreads are another way to gain clearer messages from your cards. A spread means that you are pulling multiple cards in a specific order and placing them in a certain way on the table or mat in front of you. A tarot mat can be a felt or velvet square. It doesn't need to be fancy, but having a cover for your table helps the cards to fan out evenly. This makes it easier for you to feel all of the cards and find the right one once you have your intention in your head.

Think of a spread of cards as a deeper, multifaceted answer to your question. The cards come together and tell a story. Some questions are more complicated than others, so we pull a few cards, each one with a task to help us find the insight we're searching for. In this book, you'll find a collection of three-card, four-card, five-card, and eight-card spreads, as well as a versatile spread method based on numerology. You'll also find additional spreads in the *Practical Tarot* deck guidebook as well.

Past, Present, Future

{THREE CARDS}

As your confidence grows, you can expand into a three-card reading: past, present, and future. The first card, on the left, reflects on or unveils something about your past. The second card, in the middle, focuses on the present situations in your life, and the third and final card, on the right, gives you a glimpse into your future. This is a simple, yet powerful, spread and a great place to start. Remember your intention when drawing each card. Shuffle the deck, spread the cards, and pull for "What do I need to know about my past?" then "What do I need to know about my present moment?" and finally, "What do I need to know about my future?"

Here are more complex tarot spreads to try.

New Moon Spread

{FOUR CARDS}

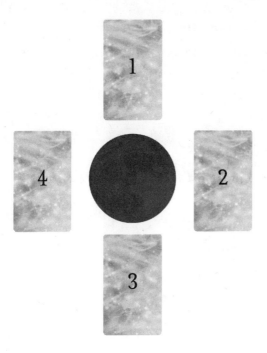

The New Moon Spread represents a new cycle beginning. You can use this during the new moon phase or anytime you need a fresh start.

- Card 1 **(Where You Are Now)**: This card will ground you in the present moment. By understanding your starting point, you'll be able to recognize your progress.

- Card 2 **(Where to Shift Your Focus)**: This will be your direction to show you where to begin this new cycle.

Card 3 (**Action to Take**): This will be your first step into this new cycle. Take action to set the transformation in motion.

Card 4 (**Inspiration**): This card will be your core message from the Universe to stay inspired during this new cycle of growth.

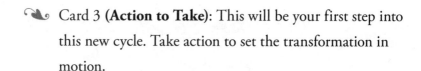

Full Moon Spread

{FOUR CARDS}

The Full Moon Spread represents a release as the moon cycle comes to completion from the new moon to full. This may be a time when you have completed a project or reached a new dream, or you might be releasing stagnant energy to prepare to begin again. You can use this spread during the full moon phase or anytime you are struggling to release pent-up worry or frustration.

- Card 1 (**What Is No Longer Serving You**): When you feel stuck or burnt out, it can be difficult to recognize what is draining your energy. This card can help you identify the culprit.

- Card 2 (**How You Can Release It**): This card will guide you to take the first step in freeing yourself from the stagnant energy that has been weighing you down.

- Card 3 (**What You've Learned**): Making mistakes or growing out of something that used to bring you joy is nothing to feel shame or guilt about. Discovering what it showed you can release the negativity and offer gratitude for the lesson.

- Card 4 (**What You've Completed since the New Moon**): Taking time to reflect on your progress and lessons you've learned along the way are important steps toward growth and gratitude for the blessings now entering your life.

Manifesting Spread

{FOUR CARDS}

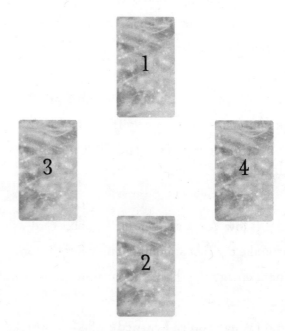

This is a great spread to use anytime you need to feel inspired or when you feel a little lost and you need clarity about how to move forward again.

🍂 Card 1 **(How can I attract my dream with my mindset? [Air]):** This card gives you the chance to get out of your own way and allow the Universe to give you some direction and clarity for your thought process and attitude.

Card 2 (**Where should I invest my time and treasure? [Earth]**): Here is your chance to invest in yourself and your dreams in a new way.

Card 3 (**How can I bring more joy into my manifesting journey? [Water]**): Think of this card as your emotional guide. Remember, we want to keep our vibration up to attract even more joyful events.

Card 4 (**What skill do I need to master? [Fire]**): This is the action you can take right now to start making forward progress again.

X-Wing Spread

{FIVE CARDS}

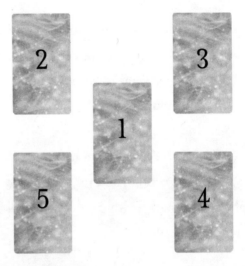

This is a powerful spread to focus on a goal and determine how you can support your progress across many areas of your life. It can also reveal your fears and blocks.

- Card 1 **(Goal/Center)**: This is the "heart" of your question, advising you what goal you may want insight into right now.

- Card 2 **(Health)**: This card suggests how your health plays into the goal or how you can physically support your goal.

- Card 3 **(Money)**: This card reveals how your finances are affecting your progress to reach your goal or what you need to know about your current financial situation in relation to your goal.

Card 4 **(Home)**: This card shines a light on ways you can create a sanctuary/safe space to manifest your goal or show how your home life is affecting your progress.

Card 5 **(Obstacle/Fear)**: This card reveals what is holding you back from your goal or what you need to overcome to reach your goal.

Maya Pyramid Spread

{EIGHT CARDS}

The Mayas built step pyramids all over Mesoamerica. The massive structures were meticulously placed to capture the sun during the solstice and equinox. This spread provides a solid foundation of your strengths to overcome the obstacles and reach the dream at the top of the pyramid.

If you are feeling overwhelmed or have faced a setback, the Maya Pyramid Spread can illuminate what's holding you back and offer ideas to break through these barriers. It can also be an encouraging spread by focusing more on your strengths (cards 5–8) than challenges (cards 2–4).

- Card 1 (**Goal**): Think of this card as the "heart" of your greatest dream or specific goal you are focusing on.

- Cards 2–4 (**Obstacles**): These cards represent events and aspects of yourself that could be holding you back.

- Cards 5–8 (**How to Overcome the Obstacles**): These cards suggest talents and activities you can tap into to inspire yourself to push past the fears and obstacles to achieve your dream. Lean into these attributes and grow.

Numerology Spreads

Your personal lucky numbers, angel numbers, and birth date numbers can lead to powerful card insights. Instead of a traditionally defined spread, you are using important numbers.

First, shuffle and fan out your deck, then count the cards. For example, my favorite numbers are 3, 8, and 13. When I want a quick "What do I need to know right now?" three-card spread, I will often reach for the third, eighth, and thirteenth cards. If you're drawing for insight into your home, try pulling cards to match your street address. If angels keep sending you numbers such as 444 or 11:11

on a clock, try shuffling the cards and pulling the fourth or eleventh card, then shuffle and pull the fourth or eleventh card again. This technique is very accurate, just remember to set an intention before pulling your numbers/cards.

These are just a handful of the many tarot spreads available, and you can also create your own. The options are limitless. Remember, your intention for each card or group of cards is always the key to your reading. Keep it simple. It doesn't take very many cards to gain clarity. Three- to five-card spreads can easily provide deeper insight without being overwhelming.

How to Do a Reading for Another Person

While this book is mainly focused on your personal connection to the cards and practical uses for tarot in everyday life, you might also be drawn to read for others. This takes practice, and as you start your tarot journey, it is best to start with a smaller three-card spread like the Past, Present, Future spread.

Unlike pulling cards for yourself, when reading tarot for another person, each spread can be interpreted in various ways depending on what you notice first when turning over the cards. It's crucial to trust that your first impression is the message for your friend or client. Deliver the message without any second-guessing. Remember, the more you allow your ego to creep in, the more you dilute the message from the Universe.

Using tarot spreads allows your cards to communicate a clearer story, offering more detailed answers and guidance. The more you use them—and down the road, possibly create your own deck that resonates with you on a core level, just like I did with *Practical Tarot*—you will have insight and inspiration at your fingertips. In the next chapter, we'll look at practical ways to use your cards to inspire creative projects, meditations, and more.

7

Practical Uses for Tarot in Everyday Situations

Tarot decks were made to be used, not to sit on the shelf. They don't need to be saved for complex life decisions or to read for friends. Tarot is a beautiful way to take your ego out of the equation and open the communication channels with your higher self and the universal energies around you. The more you use your deck, even if it's just to decide what to watch on TV, the better you will become at trusting your intuition the moment you turn the card. The answers you seek will present themselves faster, and your personal spiritual connection to the cards will continue to grow stronger. In this chapter, you'll find practical suggestions for using tarot more often to enhance your connection with the Universe and your higher self.

Exercises for Daily Practice and Inspiration

Tarot cards can be used to inspire artistic projects like writing or painting, and they can also be used for practical, everyday situations like "What should I wear today?" If you draw with a practical intention like this, you might turn a card and notice the color, or the type of shirt or dress, etc. You would set aside any traditional meaning at that point and accept the intuitive answer that came to you when you turned the card over.

What about using tarot for something as simple as deciding what to watch at the end of the night? You might turn over The Magician and decide to look for something magical. If you pulled the King of Pentacles, you might look for something like *The Wolf of Wall Street*. It's another easy way to use your tarot deck more often and build your connection to the cards.

Here are simple, engaging questions and intentions you can use for everyday situations to get in the habit of using your tarot deck:

    What am I afraid of? This is a great way to use your deck when you find yourself procrastinating on a project. Pull a card and get to the root of the issue so that you can overcome it.

    Where should I focus my energy? If you're feeling scattered or spread too thin, reach for your tarot cards to help you find direction.

    Where can I find more joy? When stress and anxiety lower your vibration, turn to your deck to shift your gaze and fill your heart with gratitude.

    What do I need to release? If you've been drawing The Devil card lately, this is a great intention to help determine what is no longer serving you. Or maybe you continue to pull the Six of Cups, which suggests you need to stop focusing on the past so you can move into the future.

    Ask your spirit guides for a message, then run your hand over your cards and draw the card that calls to you. When you turn it, this is the advice from your guides that you need right now.

    You can also pull card spreads for the full moon and new moon (see chapter 6). The new moon ushers in new beginnings, so meditate on this intention when pulling cards. The full moon is a time for fruition and release; asking your cards what needs to be forgiven or what no longer serves you can be very insightful. If you are moved by the lunar cycle, you can also pull cards for the first quarter and third quarter moon phases.

These are a just few practical ways to use your cards each day. I encourage you to make your deck a part of your everyday life, and you'll find you have insight and inspiration at your fingertips whenever you need it.

Tarot Journaling

In chapters 4 and 5, you will have found journaling prompts for each tarot card. These were just a taste of the journaling and meditative possibilities for your deck. Have you ever bought a beautiful journal with plans to fill it with your thoughts and dreams, only to leave it empty? Sometimes when you put the pen to a blank page, your mind goes blank too.

Your tarot cards can disrupt this cycle, in the best way. Pull one or two cards with the intention of "What should I write about today?" or "Which area of my life needs a deeper look?" Don't feel as though you are restricted to the traditional card meanings. If you turn the card over, see a stream, and immediately remember a river trip you took as a child, then journal about that memory. That was why you drew that card.

Maybe you turn one over and your attention goes to the person sitting by the ocean. This may inspire the idea of planning a trip to the coast. You can journal about the logistics, what you would like to do, or where you'd like to go. This could be your opportunity to visualize your future and manifest it into your reality. Allow your tarot cards to help you get out of your own way and dream bigger.

If you're facing a challenge in your life right now, keep that obstacle in mind and draw a card with the intention of a potential solution. Then journal about how the card might impact the way you approach the situation to make positive progress forward.

Using your deck to journal to gain insight and reflection into your past, present, and future is a powerful and practical way to incorporate tarot into your everyday life.

EXERCISE

Pull one card with the intention of your inspiration for the weekend. Turn the card over and write down what you focused on first. Then check the number/name of the card. What does it mean to you? Jot down all the ideas that come to you for your weekend ahead. This could include activities, events, or tasks that need to be accomplished. There are no wrong answers. At the end of the weekend, check in with your journal. How did that card impact you?

Tarot Meditation

Similar to journaling, using tarot for meditation will enhance your connection to the Universe and expand your own psychic gifts. There are many ways to add tarot to your meditation practice, but for our purposes, I'll share two powerful techniques.

Meditation provides countless benefits to your physical and mental health. Adding it to your daily routine is proven to lower stress, enhance focus and concentration skills, improve sleep quality, reduce blood pressure, and aid your immune system. You can connect with your higher self, spirit guides, and even angels through quieting your mind and opening your crown chakra.

But many people struggle with meditation, and it's no wonder why. There are so many distractions vying for our attention and forcing us to multitask. The idea of sitting still and breathing—*just* breathing—can become overwhelming. Your tarot cards can help with this.

Get your music ready, find a comfortable spot, and pull a tarot card. When you turn it over, use the card to inspire the focus of your meditation. For example, if you pulled The Empress, you might meditate on the big dreams you would like to manifest. Allow your mind to visualize your life after the dream has become reality or ask your guides to help map out a course to reach your dreams.

{3}
The Empress

If you pull the Eight of Swords, you might meditate on areas of your life where you feel stuck or trapped. How could you remove the blindfold and find your way forward again? Meditate on that question. Watch the potential solutions unfold in your mind now that you can focus without interruptions.

Another way to incorporate tarot into your meditations is to allow your spirit guides and angels to present a card in your mind. During your meditation, envision a meeting spot, maybe a bench at the beach or a cabin in the woods, whatever resonates with you. Invite your spirit guides and angels to join you. When you feel ready, ask them to show you a tarot card in your mind's eye.

Eight of Swords

{20}
Judgement

For instance, if you're struggling to manifest a romantic relationship in your life—maybe you find yourself repeating the same mistakes—you can ask for guidance through a card. Your guides might show you the Judgement card. This card signifies answering the true calling of your heart. At first, the card might seem irrelevant to your question, but upon reflection, you find yourself inspired to volunteer for causes that matter to you. This could lead to meeting someone who shares a passion of yours, breaking the pattern of your previous relationships.

By bringing tarot into your meditation, you're allowing your higher self and the angelic realms to share solutions that may be difficult to articulate. A single card in your mind's eye can communicate a path forward that you hadn't considered before.

EXERCISE

If you aren't yet comfortable with meditation, it's okay to start slow. Try pulling a tarot card with the intention of focusing on its meaning for a short, five-minute meditation. Look at your card and observe how it makes you feel. Turn on a short piece of instrumental music, close your eyes, and visualize the card in your mind's eye. Allow the meaning to vibrate through all your chakras and whisper through your mind. When the music ends, observe how you feel. Did the time fly by? Were you able to keep your mind focused on the card? This is a fun way to begin making meditation part of your self-care routine, and your tarot deck can be your guide.

Tarot and Manifesting

When you set out to manifest changes into your life, whether your goals are material like a house, more money, or a new career, or more spiritual like more peace of mind, joy, or love, tarot cards can provide the moral support and guidance you need along the journey.

Manifesting is usually long-term, and as life throws you a few curves and obstacles along the way, it's easy to be tempted to give up. When you feel stressed, then anxiety and a scarcity mindset creep in. Your connection to Spirit becomes harder to sense, and you might feel alone and lost. At that point, your negative self-talk starts to kick in, adding to the desire to quit.

But your tarot cards can be a lifeline. In chapters 4 and 5, you may have noticed manifesting tips for each card to help you stay inspired. Pulling a card pushes your ego aside and gives you an instant connection to your higher self, unlocking your intuition. You can get validation, clarity, and encouragement, right when you need it most.

Instead of conflicts and obstacles sending you spiraling, you can reach for your deck and pull a card with a simple intention like: "What can I learn from this?" Or "What do I need to release?"

Getting that simple feedback can shift your mindset from fear into possibility.

EXERCISE

Think about what dreams or changes you'd like to manifest into your life. Shuffle your cards and ask yourself: "What's been holding me back?" Pull one card and turn it over. What did you notice first on the card? Remember to lean on your intuition. You don't have to adhere to the traditional meaning of the card. Maybe you noticed the coins on the card. Has money or scarcity mindset been blocking you from taking action? What else do you see on your card? Journal about all the ideas it's inspired. Once you have an idea of what's stopping you, pull one more card with the intention of "How do I overcome this issue?" Turn the card and journal out all the ideas that come to you. Then compare your lists. You should find both clarity of what's been tripping you up as well as inspiration for how to overcome it.

Using Tarot to Inspire Creative Projects

Creatives often struggle to silence their inner critic, leading to a loss of connection with their muse. This can lead to a halt in their artistic output. Tarot is a useful tool to bypass your ego and tap directly into your creative intuition.

Over the years, I've taught a Tarot for Writers class at conventions and in various writer's groups all over the United States. I've worked with writers who have written entire books through the guidance of their tarot cards. Characters are given fictional flesh and backstories, all by pulling tarot cards with that intention. The spreads mentioned earlier in chapter 6 can be applied to your fictional characters and scenes.

Songwriters and poets can also find inspiration in tarot cards for everything from project titles to writing stanzas and developing themes. It all comes back to intention when you draw the cards.

For example, using the intention of developing a song title, I drew The Magician and the Two of Cups. Immediately the phrase "Fated Love" came into my mind. Why don't you try this exercise and draw a couple of cards to inspire a song title?

Which song title did you come up with? The options are endless because each person will find a different answer in those two cards, and none of them are wrong. It almost feels like magic, right?

As a creative, your intuition is begging to communicate with you directly, without the influence of ego. When your conscious mind gets involved, worrying about commercial viability or the opinion of others, you cut off your clear connection with your higher self and the purity of your art becomes diluted.

If visual arts are your passion, you can use tarot as a visual cue. When you turn your card, notice what claims your full attention first: the colors on the card, the symbolism of loss or love or envy, or maybe the setting on the image.

Trust this initial, intuitive message. Don't talk yourself out of the epiphany. This is the special gift of tarot cards. Allow creativity to flow directly from your higher self onto your canvas.

EXERCISE

Let's write a tarot-inspired Haiku. Grab your deck and shuffle, then pull three cards. Each card will inspire a line. Have fun with this game and tap into your cards as creative inspiration. Remember, you don't need to use the traditional card meaning for this. If the first thing your intuition homes in on is a fish or a wolf, use it. Have fun with your cards and the inspiration they ignite.

All these techniques, from using tarot to journal and meditate, to freeing your muse with creative projects, offer insight and connection with your intuition and spiritual path. By making tarot a practical partner in your everyday life, you can add a new dimension and depth to both your creative pursuits and your relationships with yourself and others.

Conclusion

Your tarot journey is just beginning. The more you use it, the stronger your connection to the cards, and their personal meanings for you will grow. There are many metaphysical tools to help you grow on your spiritual path, but few can give you the clear messages, guidance, and validations of your tarot deck.

By making your cards part of your personal development, you can enhance your intuition, open up your psychic gifts, and manifest your biggest dreams. The cards aren't meant to be on a shelf or waiting for a friend to call and ask for a reading. Your deck can offer practical help for everyday life. The cards are your key to turning down the noise of the material world and keeping a clear channel open to your connection to the universe.

My hope is that you will turn the key. Open the door to your intuition and receive clear messages and reminders that the Universe and the Divine are with you at all times, ready to cocreate for your highest good.

Acknowledgments

Thank you to the team at Beyond Words Publishing for all your support for the *Practical Tarot* deck as well as this book, *The Practical Tarot Method: Learn to Read Tarot Intuitively*. I'm so grateful to Michele and Bailey for your insights and feedback. You made this book an intuitive adventure. And to Lindsay and the rest of the amazing team, thank you for the gorgeous covers and making the deck and book so beautiful! Finally, none of this would be possible without all my backers on Kickstarter, large and small. Thank you for believing in this project before it even existed. I couldn't have manifested it without all of you.

Thanks to you, the reader, for journeying through all the tarot cycles with me. I hope it gave you some inspiration as you continue your own unique tarot exploration. I also want to thank my author friends in the Wordmakers for all the encouragement to write this book. You inspire me!

I'm so grateful to Holly Carton for her beautiful artwork for the *Practical Tarot* deck! You took my words and made them into beautiful, intuitive images that reflect our diverse world. I enjoyed every second of designing all seventy-eight cards with you.

Finally, words can't convey my gratitude to my husband, Ken. Thank you for always believing me and for encouraging me from the moment I said, "I think I want to write a book about tarot."

I couldn't do any of this without your love and support! Thank you!

Notes

1. Franco Pratesi, "In Search of Tarot Sources," November 7, 2012, http://trionfi.com/search-tarot-sources.

2. Ronald Decker, Thierry Depaulis, and Michael Dummett, *A Wicked Pack of Cards* (New York: St. Martin's Press, 1996), 66–67.

3. "Wave Feminism and the Shaping of Tarot" by Morgan Vonder Haar in *The Forum: Journal of History* 15, no. 1 (Spring 2023): 13, https://digitalcommons.calpoly.edu/forum/vol15/iss1/4/.

4. Arthur Edward Waite, *The Pictorial Key to the Tarot: Being Fragments of a Secret Tradition Under the Veil of Divination* (New Hyde Park, NY: University Books, 1966), ix–x.

5. C. G. Jung, "Lecture V: 1 March 1933," in *Notes of the Seminar Given in 1930–1934*, ed. Mary Foote (Princeton, NJ: Princeton University Press, 1997), 1:923.

6. Asta Kallo, "Around 4 in 10 Americans Have Become More Spiritual Over Time; Fewer Have Become More Religious," Pew Research Center, January 17, 2024, https://www.pewresearch.org/short-reads/2024/01/17/around-4-in-10-americans-have-become-more-spiritual-over-time-fewer-have-become-more-religious/.

7. "Cultural Appropriation and Wellness Guide," Native Governance Center, accessed April 19, 2024, https://nativegov .org/resources/cultural-appropriation-guide/

8. Joseph Campbell, *The Hero with a Thousand Faces* (Novato, CA: New World Library, 2008), 28–30.

9. Angie Green, "Tarot for Writing: The Tarot Hero's Journey," The Simple Tarot, December 11, 2019, https://thesimpletarot.com /tarot-heros-journey/.

10. Campbell, *The Hero with a Thousand Faces*, 28–30.

About the Author

Lisa Kessler has been a professional tarot card reader for nearly twenty years, reading for clients all over the world. She's a passionate teacher of tarot and has taught her Practical Tarot courses in the United States as well as online to international audiences. Her Tarot for Writers course has been presented at writers' conferences and groups around the country to help creatives connect with their intuition through tarot cards. She also posts free weekly tarot readings on her YouTube channel.

PHOTO COURTESY OF AUTHOR

Her fascination with the metaphysical world led her to work as a docent at America's Most Haunted Residence, the Whaley House, in San Diego, where she gave tours and shared ghost stories with guests from around the globe. Her love for all things paranormal is also showcased in over forty bestselling paranormal romance novels and thrillers. You can find out more about her books at AuthorLisaKessler.com.

When Lisa's not reading tarot or writing books, she's coaching others to manifest the life of their dreams. You can learn more about her Metaphysical Manifesting at metaphysicalmanifesting.com.

About the Illustrator

Holly Carton is a fine artist and illustrator who specializes in drawing out meaning in her portraits through the use of special imagery: the Victorian language of flowers, animals, symbolism, etc. She has always been fascinated by personalities and is drawn to learn more about herself and the people around her. You can see more of her artwork at her website: www.HollyCarton.com.

PHOTO COURTESY OF ILLUSTRATOR

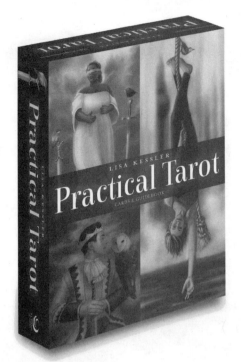

Continue your tarot journey with the companion deck.

Practical Tarot:
Cards & Guidebook

BY LISA KESSLER

THE MAJOR ARCANA

{0}

The Fool

{1}

The Magician

{2}

The High Priestess

{3}

The Empress

{4}

The Emperor

{5}

The Hierophant

{6}

The Lovers

{7}

The Chariot

{8}

Strength

{9}

The Hermit

{10}

Wheel of Fortune

{11}

Justice

{12}

The Hanged Man

{13}

Death

{14}

Temperance

{15}

The Devil

{16}

The Tower

{17}

The Star

{18}

The Moon

{19}

The Sun

{20}

Judgement

{21}

The World

THE MINOR ARCANA

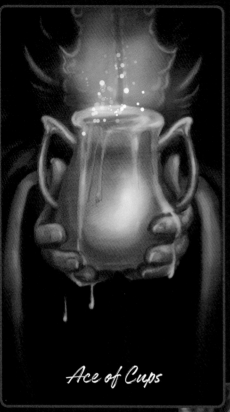

Ace of Cups

Two of Cups

Three of Cups

Four of Cups

Five of Cups

Six of Cups

Seven of Cups

Eight of Cups

Nine of Cups

Ten of Cups

Page of Cups

Knight of Cups

Queen of Cups

King of Cups

Ace of Pentacles

Two of Pentacles

Three of Pentacles

Four of Pentacles

Five of Pentacles

Six of Pentacles

Seven of Pentacles

Eight of Pentacles

Nine of Pentacles

Ten of Pentacles

Page of Pentacles

Knight of Pentacles

Queen of Pentacles

King of Pentacles

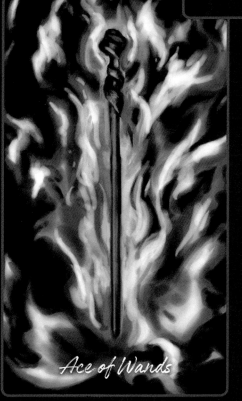

Ace of Wands

Two of Wands

Three of Wands

Four of Wands

Five of Wands

Six of Wands

Seven of Wands

Eight of Wands

Nine of Wands

Ten of Wands

Page of Wands

Knight of Wands

Queen of Wands

King of Wands

Ace of Swords

Two of Swords

Three of Swords

Four of Swords

Five of Swords

Six of Swords

Seven of Swords

Eight of Swords

Nine of Swords

Ten of Swords

Page of Swords

Knight of Swords

Queen of Swords

King of Swords